Hampton Cars

With Best Wishes

4. 11 2013

The Story of Hampton Cars.

Published by Hampton Cars, Sequoia, Tobacconist Road.

Minchinhampton.

Stroud, Glos. GL6 9JJ.

British Library Cataloguing in Publication Data:

A catalogue record for this book is available from the British Library

ISBN 0 9531672 0 8

MICHAEL SEDGWICK MEMORIAL TRUST

This work is published with the assistance of the Michael Sedgwick Memorial Trust.
Founded in memory of the well known motoring researcher and author, Michael Sedgwick (1926-1983), the Trust is a registered charity to encourage new research and the recording of motoring history.
Suggestions for future projects and donations should be sent to the
Honorary Secretary of the Michael Sedgwick Memorial Trust.Spring Cottage,
20 High Street, Milford-on-Sea, Lymington.Hampshire SO41 0QD.

Designed and produced by Terry Cripps - TCDB Design.

Colour photography by: Neill Bruce. Andrew Morland.

Additional photography by the author.

Water colour of Lifford Mills by E.W. (Bill) Cornock

Front cover picture loaned by Keith Stimson.

Printed by Cotswold Printing Co. Ltd., Stroud, Glos.

Preface

The decision to compile this book was made during the summer of 1996 when I heard that the old Dudbridge Ironworks was about to be re-developed - or, more precisely, that the old Hampton Cars factory and office block were to be demolished.

A few months earlier I had had the good fortune to read Ian Holmes' hand-written account of Hampton's history which he had prepared for a local school project in 1983 when he was just 15 years of age. Reading this and the fact that my Company had rented the very same office block between May 1986 and May 1989 somewhat focused my mind on Hamptons and was reinforced by the almost daily sight of the fast fading sign "Hampton Cars" and "Offices on Right" painted on the red brick wall of the old Works. The decision was finally cemented when the opportunity to acquire the Hampton archive material of the late Bonnie Monro presented itself almost at the same time as I was kindly given access to the extensive research material of the well known local enthusiast, the late Max Williamson. Both of these sets of information were obtained with the invaluable assistance of Keith Stimson who now owns Max's Hampton.

Bonnie and Max compared notes several times during the Sixties and were keen to share their knowledge with a wider public and Bonnie had actually prepared a manuscript entitled "The Pride and Joy of a Vintage Car". From the foregoing it is easy to understand why I have dedicated this book to their memory and hope that the result will do justice to the subject and their considerable effort. Many other people have contributed to my research and without their willing help many small details might have been omitted and for this I thank them all. Notwithstanding this assistance, however, any errors or omissions in the text must be ascribed exclusively to me.

I have visited more libraries, museums and record offices during the past few months than at any time in my life; but whilst carrying out this research I have made very many new friends and this has helped the project to flow along.

Unfortunately, our story is not a particularly happy one and there is no fairy tale ending but I would wish it to be considered as a tribute to the hard working people of Stroud who displayed considerable skill and dedication to the Hampton cause against the most difficult background of the Twenties.

When the complete industrial history of the twentieth century is written Dudbridge will have made its mark and in particular "Hampton Cars" will take their place as "Gloucestershire's only Volume Car Manufacturer".

Contents

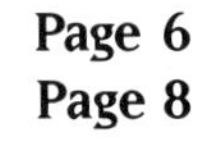

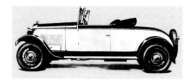

Arthur Maxwell Williamson - Gentleman

By Laurence F. Tann

1913 - 1975

Max was a gentleman and a good friend and neighbour who, apart from his family, wife Ruby and daughters Sheila, Daphne and Penny and his job as a teacher at a special school for disabled children in Gloucester, loved vintage cars and motor sport.

He had been brought up with a family background of motor cars and became addicted to motor racing following visits to Brooklands with his uncle and studying the history of the sport through books and magazines.

A long time member of The Vintage Sports Car Club (VSCC) and founder member of the Cotswold Sports Car Club, he introduced me to the sport and I have fond memories of arriving at Silverstone at 8 am to the mouth watering aroma of eggs, bacon and fried bread cooked on a primus stove.

Another favourite family outing of Max's was to Madresfield, near Malvern, for the VSCC Rally; what days they were with wonderful driving tests, beautiful picnics and an array of cars so different in design as to not only make them exciting to look at but to provide much debate about the pros and cons of many mechanical devices.

During our period of friendship Max had a number of cars; the first that I remember was a Riley 11.9 sports tourer - a little story about that car I must relate : at the bottom of my garden was a square with about 8 garages on each of two facing sides. Max occupied one in the middle of a row and had been working on the car for some weeks on a major repair to

the cone clutch. One evening about 11 o'clock I noticed a dim light coming from his garage so I wandered over to see what was happening. There was Max, candle in one hand, paint brush in the other, applying a coat of light green paint to the car body.

He had entered the car in the Concours d'Elégance of the Riley Register National Rally to be held at the original Riley Works the next day so he thought he'd smarten the car up a bit. Mixing the paint with a liberal dose of Terrabin (driers) he started, but the battery of his torch gave out so a candle was the last resort. Next morning, I was awakened by a loud crash and on investigation I saw Max looking at the back end of the Riley protruding from the doors of a thankfully empty garage on the other side of the square. He had rolled the car out of his garage, started it on the handle, stepped aside to get in, then somehow it slipped into gear and took off. We extricated the car hardly scratched but ever so slightly tacky and off he went to Coventry to win a major trophy.

An Alvis Firebird followed the Riley, then a lovely Alfa 1750 Zagato which required a lot of work and which sadly seized and cracked its block on its first test run. This was followed by an Alvis Silver Eagle, a lovely car and lastly a fully tuned Turner and boy did he drive it! Max worked on his cars, resisting help from his friends, in spite of his disablement due to contracting polio in his early 20's.

Max took a course in book binding at Stroud Technical College so that he could bind VSCC magazines for pocket money after his retirement. He did manage a few before he passed away in 1975. We all miss him - Max was a gentleman.

His bookbinding symbol

Max's Hampton rests awhile outside the factory in 1953

Bonnie Monro - The Lady with the Hampton
by Brian Joscelyne

1927 - 1993

I first met Bonnie, whose real name was Elaine, through her elder brother Alastair. We were students together in the early fifties at London University. Being at the same college we shared a passion for vintage cars - he had a 1928 Morris Oxford and I had a 1938 2 litre Aston Martin.

The Morris had a dickey seat so we piled in as many friends as we could and off we would go to Silverstone or Brands Hatch and hope we would get home again !

Later Alastair had a Blackburne-engined Frazer Nash in which we had many adventures together. Whenever I went to visit the Monros I was always made to feel part of the family and when Alastair got married I was his best man. His sisters, Bonnie and Jean, never married.

The family had Scottish connections and for many years Mrs. Monro held a high position in the Royal household of Queen Mary.

Mr. Monro was head of one of the largest firms operating in Covent Garden vegetable market. They married in 1921 and lived in Hampton where Bonnie was born in 1927. In 1930 they moved to Broadwater Lodge which was the family home for 59 years. Situated at Oatlands village mid-way between Walton-on-Thames and Weybridge it is not surprising that Brooklands was to feature in their lives especially after the Brooklands Society was formed in 1967.

Bonnie was educated privately in Walton-on-Thames and after several moves eventually became Head Girl at Sarum Girls' School. On leaving, she entered the teaching profession progressing from kindergarten level, to Westward School and finally to Senior Mistress at Danesfield. After 42 years dedicated to education she retired and moved with her sister Jean to live at Ferring in Sussex in 1989.

My personal memories of Bonnie were of an outgoing and ever cheerful personality with a ready ability to get on with everybody. Her interests were many and included spinning and weaving, sharing a workshop with Jean making rugs and covers of all kinds. Bonnie had a great gift of colour blending and pattern designing for a wide variety of hand-woven articles. The two sisters were also skilled at creating soft toys of all kinds. These were sold at Agricultural and Craft Shows to raise money for Cancer Research. Bonnie also ran a popular Scottish Dancing Group in Oatlands village as well as participating in big Scottish Dance evenings in the West End of London.

With this background it was something of a surprise to find Bonnie's real interest in old cars. She got it from Alastair of course and it was he who helped her to acquire HW 2734 in 1961 which she owned and enjoyed for 32 years. It was the only one of the marque in continuous active use. Soon after buying the Hampton she enrolled at Brooklands Technical College for a car maintenance course. From then on Bonnie kept it going entirely herself apart from helpful advice from Alastair and later John Granville Grenfell. Thereafter, she took the car all over Southern England including visits to Dudbridge, the car's birthplace, where she made friends with several of the Hampton workforce who were pleased to give her first hand information for her planned book. She was an enthusiastic and active member of the Vintage Sports Car Club.

Bonnie died after much suffering on March 6th 1993 at the Royal Marsden Hospital. Jean and I promised her that somehow her Hampton researches would be put to good use and I am extremely grateful to the author for making this possible.

The Monro's at Brooklands 60th Anniversary - June 1967. Alastair, Jean, Marjorie and Bonnie.

I

The Early Days - Before the Great War

1914 Early Hampton with temporary bodywork descending Nailsworth Ladder.

Our story opens at the turn of the century when interest in the horseless carriage was gathering momentum.

Weigel Grand Prix Racing Car. Circuit Des Ardennes 1907

Danny Weigel was the successful managing director of Clement-Talbot until 1905 when he set up his own company Weigel Motors Ltd., at Goswell Street in the City of London. During the next few years he produced 25/40/60 hp cars in small numbers but is best remembered for his venture into Grand Prix racing cars with large straight eight engines - though with little success. It certainly did not impress his bank manager so he re-structured the Company in 1907 and moved to Notting Hill. Further financial difficulties followed, resulting in the sale of the company to Albert Crowdy who created a new organisation called Crowdy Ltd. in November 1909. It is interesting to note that the vendor of the business was Thomas Faulkner from Fairford in Gloucestershire and not Weigel himself. It seems that motoring pioneers generally used other people's money - a situation which prevails throughout our story.

CROWDY·LTD
Successors to
WEIGEL MOTORS·1907 LTD
TELEPHONE: 4091 WESTERN

THE RED MARK

OLAF STREET
LATIMER·ROAD
NOTTING·HILL
LONDON·W
TELEGRAMS: WEIGELMOTO. LONDON

It appears that Crowdy used some Weigel design features plus ideas of his own in creating his cars during 1910/11 but reference to his letterhead reveals two things. First, Weigel Motors is mentioned; secondly, he uses a trade mark taking the form of a triangle similar to Alvis with the wording "The Red Mark". Is it a coincidence that in 1914 a similar red triangle with its base at the bottom also appears on a later Hampton brochure ?

Reference to his 1910 brochure reveals the use of Hewitt piston valve engines (for which Crowdy held a licence) and full details of four models.

A whole range of bodies was offered from the modest two seater phaeton Torpedo with dashboard radiator at £75 to the six seater (2+2+2) Landaulette at £250.

It is perhaps sobering to note that they were ahead of their time in offering a 3 year guarantee and parts availability for 5 years - sadly they were not around long enough to test the validity of this rather bold promise. Crowdy also patented a tyre security wing nut which sold for 12 shillings (60p) for a car set of 16.

	Engine	Gearbox	Chassis Price
19hp TWO SEATER DE LUXE,	Hewitt 4 Cyl.		
Wheelbase 9 feet 6 inches.	89mm x 120 mm	3 speed	£425.
29hp CAR DE LUXE,	Hewitt		
Wheelbase a) 10 feet 9 inches	6 Cyl.	3 speed	£600.
b) 11 feet 9 inches	89mm x 127mm		£625.
30hp TORPEDO			
Wheelbase a) 9 feet 6 inches	4 Cyl.	4 speed	£450.
c) 10 feet 6 inches	110mm x 120mm		£475.
This model was the only one to use 3/4" elliptical rear suspension.			
39hp CABRIOLET			
Wheelbase a) 9 feet 11 inches	4 Cyl.	4 speed	£550.
b) 10 feet 9 inches	127mm x 140mm		£575.

Weigel 1908/09 with "Roi Des Belges" body made by Barker for Frank Cayley.

Later in the autumn of 1911 Crowdy was on the move to West Heath Works, Northfield, some eight miles south of Birmingham. West Heath was also the author's home from 1939 to 1964. Albert Crowdy rented a most interesting building from Mrs. Clara Pegram which had been purpose built two years previously: namely, "The Northfield Skating Rink and Winter Garden" which had failed to cash in on the then popular leisure pursuit of roller skating. At the original opening, Mr. J.W. Jacques, the resident instructor, gave a sparkling skating display accompanied by The Northfield Institute Prize Band - the very same brass band with which a twelve year old Trevor Picken commenced his musical career in 1946 playing third cornet.

Surely Crowdy must have been the only British car manufacturer to build his cars on a surface of "maple wood which rested upon a layer of felt supported

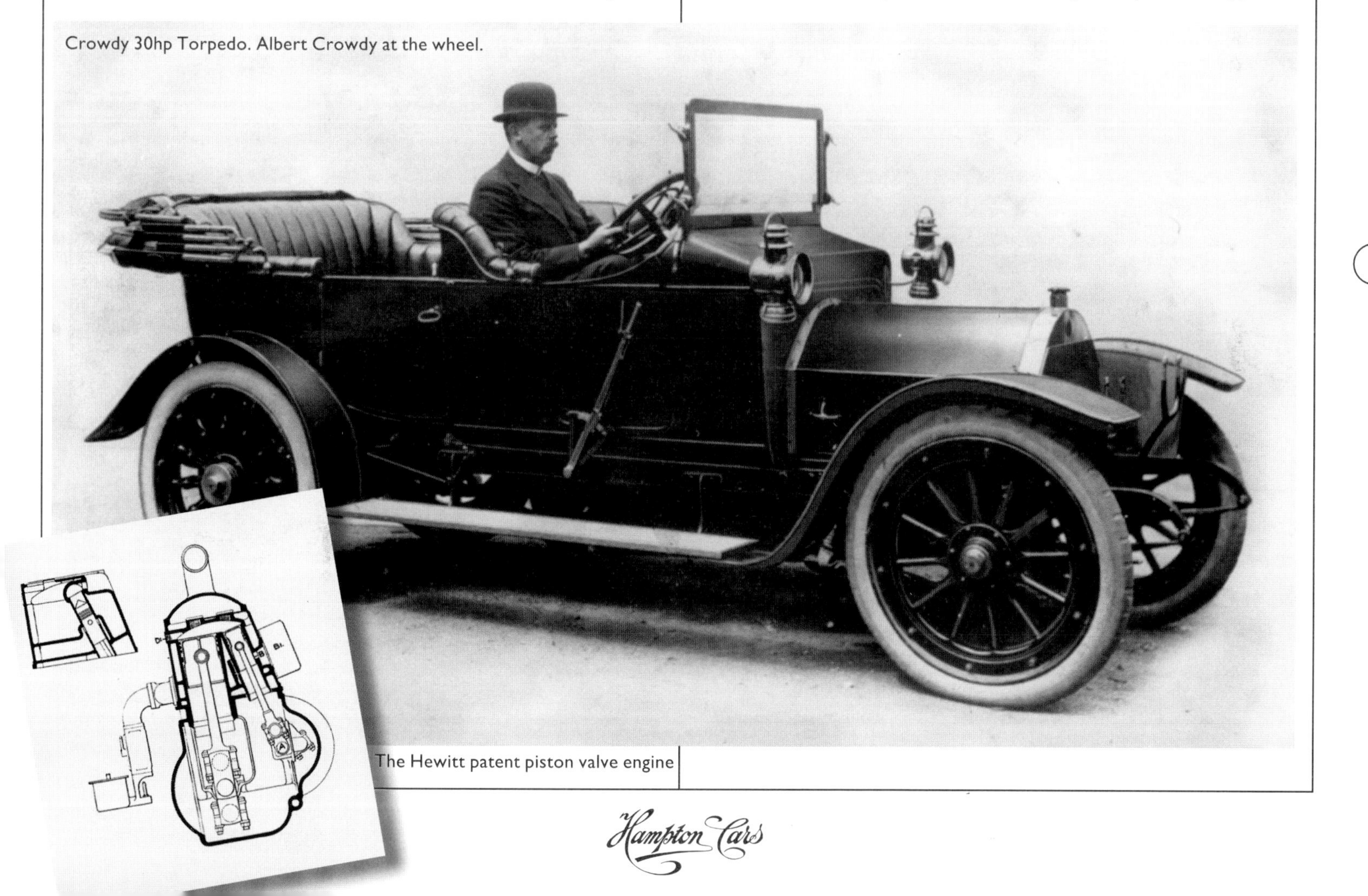

Crowdy 30hp Torpedo. Albert Crowdy at the wheel.

The Hewitt patent piston valve engine

upon a seasoned pine base". These premises were but 200 yards from the Northfield Station of the Liverpool & Manchester Railway.

The reasons for this dramatic move to Birmingham are not clear but one suspects financial pressure from the original vendor, who held a substantial debenture. On the positive side let us consider the advantages: the large

Crowdy Ltd., West Heath Road, Northfield, Birmingham.
The River Rea runs under the bridge with the factory 50 yards to the left of the photographer's viewpoint.

number of component manufacturers and sub-contractors available to him in Birmingham; the proximity of the Longbridge Works of Herbert Austin (with his labour force of 1,000) which could have provided trained motor engineers; and, if required, an additional source of both men and materials was available in Coventry, only 23 miles to the east.

After only a few months, however, the move to West Heath had not averted disaster and on 27th February 1912 Edward Wells from London was appointed Receiver by Thomas Faulkner. In May the assets were sold and by September new directors were installed and the Company moved its registered office to Lifford Mill, Kings Norton, some two miles closer to Birmingham. The new owners were Lewis Radmore (Chairman) and William Miller (Secretary) who lived at "Wallaford", Meriden Road, Hampton-in-Arden, Warwickshire. In what appears to have been a complicated deal, they used Crowdy Ltd. to take over a private venture financed by Tulloch & Co. (Shippers) who used the name, Hampton Engineering Company (not limited). It seems that whilst negotiations were going on Tulloch became bankrupt !

Hampton Engineering had been experimenting with motor cycles and cyclecars for at least a year under the direction of William Paddon, possibly from premises near Hampton-in-Arden. How Paddon, who had previously been involved with Arrol-Johnson in Scotland and Standard Motors of Coventry, met up with Radmore and Miller is not known but as Coventry was close to Hampton-in-Arden where Miller lived, perhaps they were friends or neighbours. As Radmore and Miller were keen golfers it is also possible that they met him in the bar of the The North Warwickshire Golf Club (formerly Hampton-in-Arden Golf Club) where they were active members.

Albert Moore was one of the first employees at Lifford Mill in 1911, having learnt his trade as a patternmaker at

"Wallaford",
Hampton-in-Arden, Warwickshire.

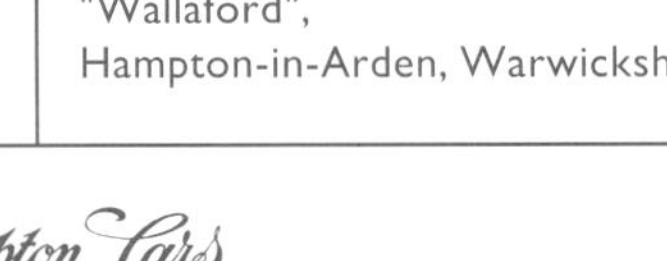

DUPLICATE FOR THE FILE

No. 105666

Certificate of Change of Name.

I hereby Certify, That the

Crowdy Limited

having, with the sanction of a **Special Resolution** of the said Company, and with the approval of the BOARD OF TRADE, changed its name, is now called the

Hampton Engineering Company, Limited

and I have entered such new name on the Register accordingly.

Given under my hand at London, this *Thirty-first* day of *December* One Thousand Nine Hundred and *thirteen*

Assistant Registrar of Joint Stock Companies.

Certificate received by

Date *2 Jan 1914.*

Lifford Mills, Kings Norton, Worcestershire. (Later Birmingham)

Hampton Engineering Co. Ltd. 2nd January 1914. The formal name change.

Is the one you are looking for.
ENGINE, 85 Bore and 88 Stroke.
Bosch Magneto.
B. & B. Carburetter.
Brooks Saddle B104.
Free Engine Hub.
Hutchinsons Tyres.
Saxon Forks.
Radmill Lamp and Generator.
Foot Pump.
Horn.
Toolbag and Tools.
WATFORD Speedometer.
COMPLETE.
THERE ARE NO EXTRAS.
The HAMPTON ENGINEERING Co., LIFFORD MILLS, KING'S NORTON,
will gladly send you full particulars.

This advertisement appeared in "The Motor Cycle" 28th Nov 1912)

Albert Henry Moore's character reference from B.S.A.

TELEGRAMS: "SMALLARMS, BIRMINGHAM." TELEPHONE: 6440 CENTRAL (6 LINES).

THE BIRMINGHAM SMALL ARMS COMPANY LIMITED

Any reply should be addressed to the Company and this reference quoted:

N/KW.

TRADE MARKS.

B.S.A.

Birmingham

REDDITCH.

August 12th 1910.

TO THOSE CONCERNED

We hereby certify that A.E. Moore was in the employ of this Company about 9 years. During that period we found him honest, sober, good timekeeper, and good workman.

THE BIRMINGHAM SMALL ARMS CO LTD.

H. Nicholls

WORKS MANAGER.

The Birmingham Small Arms Co. Ltd. (B.S.A.) in Redditch. His experience gained there would have enabled him to make a useful contribution to the design of the Hampton motor cycle. Martin Fussey, a designer, is the only other employee who can be identified from the Kings Norton period.

The Old Mill at Lifford was rented by Radmore and Miller from George Griffin and had been empty for at least fifteen years but certainly had a colourful industrial history in the nineteenth century. It is believed to have been originally a corn mill before Thomas Dobbs operated a metal rolling mill there in the early part of the century but by 1860 it was converted to the production of rubber goods until 1896. It was during this period that other buildings were added to the original mill, now covering most of the site, although the original 14 foot water wheel was still in situ. Detailed research has been carried out on this site which indicates it was probably in a poor state when Crowdy/Hampton moved in during the middle of 1912. Prior to the First World War there were many entrepreneurs assembling motor cycles and cyclecars from proprietary components in the Midlands so Hampton's activities were typical and a normal prelude to more serious motor car production. For example only half a mile from Lifford Mill in Franklin Road, Kings Norton, Mr. J.L. Edwards was offering his Touring and Brooklands cyclecars with 8hp Precision engine at £95 and Mr. F.N. Hail was producing a commercial traveller's cyclecar for £75 at nearby Hockley Brook. The pattern seemed to be to produce a viable prototype, follow that with a press release and hope this would result in enough sales to assist with the further development of the product. Our surviving motor cycle comes from this period. The details of one of Paddon's cyclecars was reported in The Cyclecar in February 1913 as follows :

The Hampton Cars factory at Lifford Mill. The River Rea also flowed past their door as it had at Northfield.

The Pattern Shop, Lifford Works, circa 1913. Albert Moore was given this photograph by William Paddon. It had been "re-touched" for use in a leaflet.

Motor cycles and cyclecars of the 1912 period meeting at "Ye Stonebridge Hotel & Petrol Station".

The ten ton waterwheel prior to its removal in 1952.

THE HAMPTON CYCLECARS

"The most notable feature of the Hampton cyclecar, just introduced, is the exceedingly long belts. The power unit is an 8hp air-cooled twin Precision and directly coupled to it is the gearbox, giving three speeds forward, the gear being the well known D.H.K. A 7/16 inch by 3/4 inch pitch chain transmits the power to the countershaft and thence the drive to the back wheels is by 12 feet long 1 inch V belts. A Bosch magneto and Amac two-lever type carburettors are fitted, while lubrication is by the Best and Lloyd forced-feed system. Under the scuttle dash is the petrol tank with a generous capacity of four gallons which is estimated to be sufficient fuel for 200 miles. The pedal on the left controls the clutch, while the right hand pedal operates the foot brake, which works on the countershaft. A hand brake of the contracting band type also works on the back wheels. The frame is constructed of channel steel and is very light as numerous holes have been drilled in it wherever the metal could be spared. A two-seater torpedo body is fitted as standard and a comfortable driving position is obtained by the steering wheel being slightly raked. Another model will shortly be manufactured which will be fitted with a water-cooled Precision engine and will have a worm-driven back axle. In other respects it will be identical with the foregoing and will sell at about £115 while the cheaper model will be offered at £80."

At an AGM. on 25th November 1913 the Company name was changed to : THE HAMPTON ENGINEERING CO. LTD. using the same Company number 105666 as created by Crowdy and situated at Lifford Mill, Kings Norton. However, on 21st October 1914 the registered office was changed to London House, Crutched Friars, London E.C. This was the address of Arthur Wright who was associated with Tulloch & Co. but on 7th May 1915 this was reversed and the registered office returned to Lifford Mill.

The amalgamation of the Crowdy Company and Paddon's Hampton Engineering and their various products into Lifford Mill appears to have been a recipe for success. In January 1914 a light car was offered at 150 guineas (£157.50) and The Light Car & Cyclecar reported : "The great feature of the car is undoubtedly the engine which is a two-stroke two cylinder. After some fairly extensive tests, the makers have come to the conclusion that the two-stroke is,

"Ye Stonebridge Hotel" 1930. 2 miles from Hampton-in-Arden close to the junction of the busy A45/A446 roads.

on account of its simplicity and low first cost, the best engine for light car work". This was yet another in the series of confusing press announcements to add to others which mentioned various engine sizes including a 65mm x 100mm 4 cylinder side valve and 60mm x 110mm 4 cylinder Chapuis-Dornier. The variations in track and wheelbase measurements were almost as great but only seem to confirm that Hampton were still trying to finalise a good design with which to impress their potential customers. It is the author's view that towards the end of 1913 the Company had completed their product development phase and that the specification of the vehicle described in some detail in their 1914 brochure was their first significant production car. This of course had a 4 cylinder water cooled side valve engine despite the odd statement regarding the air cooled twin engine - perhaps the Press misunderstood or were rather late in printing an old report. The new model was priced at £295 - a real motor car at last.

Unfortunately, there is little evidence that any major features or components of the Crowdy were incorporated into the 1914 Hamptons with the possible exception of the rear springing. The first ascents of Nailsworth Ladder come from this period and are detailed later in our story. The only item that came from West Heath to Lifford Mill was their telegraphic address "Silence", perhaps indicating the opposite of noisy roller skates.

Two Extraordinary General Meetings were held in quick succession in June and July 1914, chaired by Lewis Radmore, at which time the authorised capital of the Company was increased to £50,000.

William Miller left the Board and presumably the Company. Two new directors were appointed - Arthur Wright (of Tulloch & Co., the previous financiers) and Charles Apperly of Stroud. This information was not registered, however, until October 1914 which suggests some irregularities. However, war was declared in August 1914, production stopped and subsequently the factory closed.

William Paddon issued a notice to his workforce on the lst August which said: "Owing to the extreme gravity of the International situation in Europe and the consequent difficulty of obtaining sufficient gold to pay wages etc., from the Banks, as all Banks are now held up for supplies of gold, we may find it necessary to close these Works for an indefinite period as from Monday next, but hope that such will not be the case.

"We will advise all men later when they are to recommence work. In the meantime, we are closing down these Works as from Monday next until the Monday following, provided fresh difficulties in the situation should not have arisen. Should these arise the Works will be closed indefinitely as above stated, and all employees must accept this in lieu of the usual notice." He followed this with a letter in September to Albert Moore in which he explained the latest

continued on Page 24

Codes: A.B.C. 5th.
Liebers.

The Hampton Engineering Co. Ltd.

Telephone: 174 King's Norton.
Telegrams & Cables: "SILENCE, King's Norton."

LIFFORD MILLS,
LIFFORD, BIRMINGHAM.

Station: LIFFORD STATION.
(Midland Railway.)

Hampton Four Seater Torpedo, complete - £295

Hampton Cars Are constructed under the best possible conditions—in a large, airy factory, replete with every facility for the rapid and accurate production of a high grade Car at a competitive price. Abundant water power is available, with rail and canal transport systems right at the door, whilst the comfort and health of the workers is materially improved by the ideal surroundings in which the factory is situated.

Extracts from Hampton's first brochure. 1914.

One Model only 12-16 h.p.   Chassis Price £250

SPECIFICATION.

Chassis. Frame of pressed steel. Front Springs ½ elliptic, Rear ¾ elliptic, very long. Grease Cups fitted to same.

Engine. 12-16 h.p., Four Cylinders cast en bloc, 75 × 130. Enclosed Valves, Adjustable Tappets.

Cooling. Thermo - syphon with Radiator and Fan. Special allowance made for hot climates.

Lubrication. Forced Feed Lubrication to every engine bearing by pump in sump—Indicator on dash.

Carburetter. Zenith Automatic.

Chassis side view shewing Gear box, Gate control, and Dynamo drive.

Magneto. High Tension Bosch. Watertight enclosed.

Clutch. Leather to metal, extremely light.

Gear Box. Three Speeds and Reverse. Ball bearings throughout. Gate change.

Universal Joints. Special Hampton design, enclosed in oil retaining covers.

Transmission. Bevel Drive, specially strong, mounted on ball bearings with ball thrusts. The Wheels are mounted on outer sleeves, so that the differential shafts carry no weight. Specially high clearance for rough roads.

Brakes. Foot and Side Brakes, metal to metal, internal expanding, enclosed in dust-proof drums, both actuating on the back wheels. Thus no brake strain comes on transmission.

Steering. Worm and Sector, irreversible.

Control. By Accelerator Pedal.

Front Axle of H Section Steel, very strong; Steering Swivels, mounted on Ball Thrusts making steering extremely light to handle

Wheels. 760 × 90, Sankey Steel, interchangeable. Spare Wheel.

Tyres. 760 × 90. Dunlop.

The brochure also gave the following information :

	Standard chassis	Colonial model
Wheelbase	9 foot 0 inches	9 foot 6 inches
Track	4 foot 3 inches	4 foot 8 inches

ENGINE

Monobloc Casting; four cylinders, 75 m m. × 130 m/m.; extra large bearings of special alloy; bearings fed with oil under pressure from force pump in crank chamber sump, so regulated that the amount of oil is directly proportional to the work being done by the engine—any excess oil escaping through a pressure relief valve—thus **ensuring perfect and continuous lubrication and a smokeless exhaust.** An oil pressure gauge is fitted on dashboard in front of driver. All valves arranged on one side of engine, of extra large diameter, enclosed with the operating mechanism in a dust-tight aluminium cover, the design making for both cleanliness and silence. The water jacketing of the cylinders is particularly efficient; the cooling of the cylinder heads and valve pockets having received special attention.

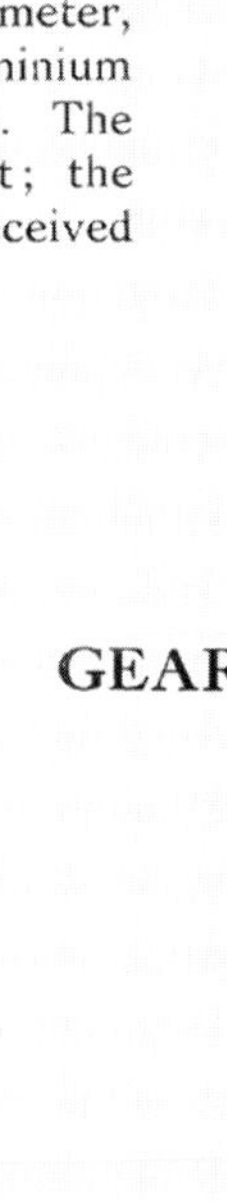

GEAR BOX

The Gear Box is a one-piece aluminium casting, so constructed as to be oil-tight, and provided with adjustable packing glands. Gears are mounted on nickel steel castellated shafts which in their turn are supported by combined ball and roller bearings. The direct drive or top gear is by means of an internally cut gear, this considerably shortening the length of shaft otherwise necessary, and making the gear changing operation absolutely simple and easy.

The primary and lay shafts are mounted one above the other, thus materially reducing the width of the box, and by reason of the lower shaft and gears being immersed in oil, results in thorough lubrication of the gears, and consequent reduction in noise.

and the "**Hampton**" universal joint of the "ring and stud" type is equal to any on the market. Every part is interchangeable and renewable, should wear take place, and heavy bushes of special bearing metal, well supplied with lubricant, ensure a minimum of friction and consequent loss of power. Both joints are wholly enclosed in neat and readily detachable brass covers, with leather extensions which retain the oil. The substantial construction of these universal joints will be evident on examination of illustrations.

HAMPTON REAR AXLE, with cover plate removed, for inspection of driving bevel and differential gear.

REAR AXLE

This is of special design, so constructed that the gears and driving shafts, together with the whole of the differential, may be taken down without removing the axle from the car, and the whole of the gears may be inspected at any time by simply removing a cover plate, which exposes the whole of the internal mechanism to view. This construction enables a change of gear ratio to be made at any time

REAR AXLE, showing method of removing driving bevel and differential unit for inspection.

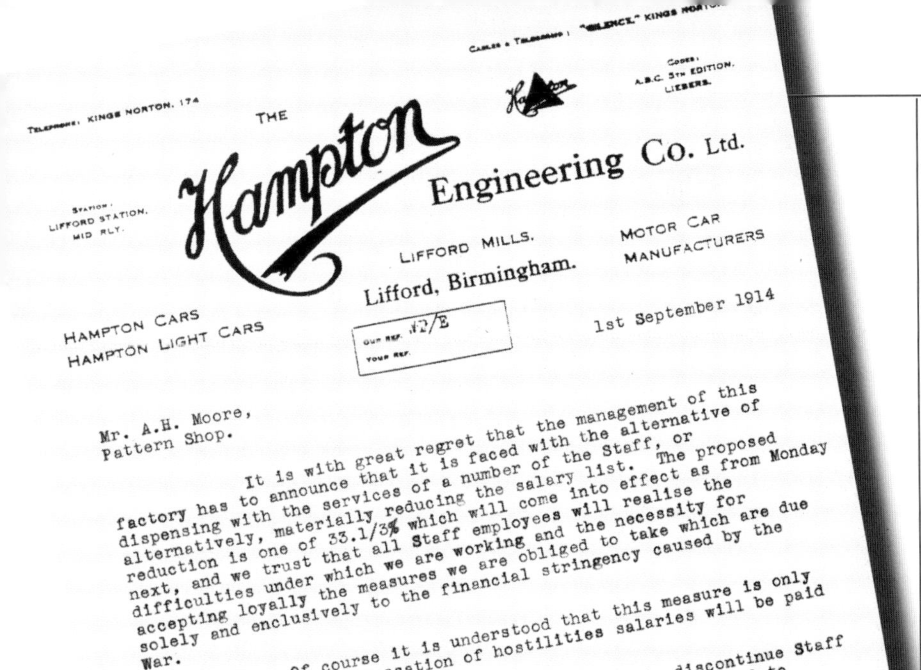

TELEPHONE: KINGS NORTON. 174

CABLES & TELEGRAMS: "SILENCE," KINGS NORTON.

CODES: A.B.C. 5TH EDITION. LIEBERS.

THE Hampton Engineering Co. Ltd.

STATION: LIFFORD STATION, MID RLY.

LIFFORD MILLS. Lifford, Birmingham.

MOTOR CAR MANUFACTURERS

HAMPTON CARS
HAMPTON LIGHT CARS

OUR REF. WP/E
YOUR REF.

1st September 1914

Mr. A.H. Moore,
Pattern Shop.

It is with great regret that the management of this factory has to announce that it is faced with the alternative of dispensing with the services of a number of the Staff, or alternatively, materially reducing the salary list. The proposed reduction is one of 33.1/3% which will come into effect as from Monday next, and we trust that all Staff employees will realise the difficulties under which we are working and the necessity for accepting loyally the measures we are obliged to take which are due solely and enclusively to the financial stringency caused by the War.

Of course it is understood that this measure is only temporary and on the cessation of hostilities salaries will be paid at the usual rate.

We also regret that we shall have to discontinue Staff Teas, those of the Staff who require a cup of tea are asked to obtain same from the Tea Room adjoining the works.

FOR THE HAMPTON ENGINEERING CO. LTD.

W. Paddon

GENERAL MANAGER

situation, perhaps minimising its seriousness. His final sentence regarding the withdrawal of tea is difficult to comprehend, bearing in mind the Country was now at war, but the "Tea Room" on the other side of Tunnel Lane still survives today as a refreshment room despite the fact that the factory was demolished in 1953. The British, it seems, cannot manage without their tea.

Later, it is known that Arthur Wright with Ralph Ward formed a new limited company called Tulloch & Co. Ltd. on 15th December 1914 (buying the remains of their old shipping organisation, Tulloch & Co.) with a nominal capital of £30,000. They became joint managing directors for life but as they leave the Hampton scene it is necessary to note that Tulloch went into voluntary receivership on lst May 1915 and was finally wound up in September 1917. The haven of a limited liability company was probably their real objective.

Lewis Radmore, however, joined the Royal Naval Air Service and rose to the rank of Flight Sub Lieutenant before being killed in action on 6th September 1916. He was buried at Hampton-in-Arden. (Recorded on the village war memorial.)

General Manager, William Paddon, also joined HM. Forces and "rendered valuable services connected with the establishment and equipment of many

Picture from brochure shows forward mounted headlights.

Arthur Harrison at the wheel of his 1914 two seater Torpedo Hampton.
He worked at "The Royal Oak", Wineham in West Sussex.

Government munitions factories". Apperly continued to direct his Gloucestershire based industries some of which were engaged in war production.

In October 1915, Arthur Russell was appointed Receiver and Manager of Hampton Engineering Co. Ltd. by a Debenture holder, (probably Arthur Wright) and subsequently discharged in August 1917. This Company was formally dissolved in December 1918 just one month after the end of World War One. Regrettably, the intervention of the war had snuffed out the promising Hampton Car enterprise and whilst a solitary motor cycle survives, we do not have any cars from this period to evaluate. As factory records did not survive the war, we can only guess at how many vehicles were turned out by their two dozen strong work force. Perhaps during their two year occupation of Lifford Mill they made 50 or so vehicles. Finally, whilst William Paddon was making his important contribution to the war effort, one wonders if the drawings and designs of his cars were safely secreted at the bottom of his briefcase.

2

Meanwhile, back at the Dudbridge Ironworks

Salmson (Canton-Unné) water cooled aero engine.

Dudbridge lies one mile west of Stroud and is a small compact area surrounded by Cainscross, Rodborough, Selsley and Lightpill. The name dates from before 1234 AD and its medieval bridge is at the junction of the Nailsworth and Frome Valleys.

In addition, three turnpike roads, the Stroudwater Canal and a Branch Line Railway (LMS) all passed very close. It is sufficient to say that good communications were well established in the nineteenth century which helps to explain why it became a significant engineering area. Historically, the Stroud Valleys were dominated by the wool and cloth processing industries with a wide variety of mills powered by water from the fast flowing streams. These textile activities naturally attracted many ancillary industries including woodworking, pin manufacturing, brick making, rubber products and a variety of engineering based businesses which were essential for the maintenance of the machinery used in the mills.

Our story begins at a time when many of the traditional textile mills were seeking to diversify and to look for new business opportunities for the twentieth century - mainly in the field of engineering.

The Dudbridge Ironworks Ltd. was formed in December 1899 by the directors of Humpidge, Holborow and Co. Ltd. who had been trading under various

1895 T. Graves-Smith J.D. Humpidge H.T. Humpidge The Directors are standing by the rear doorway of their office block. The main door looked out onto Selsley Hill.

The stonework surrounding these historic entrances has been re-built into Sainsbury's wall - a plaque explains their significance.

These doorways belonged to a clothier's house which lay close to this site and was demolished at the end of the 19th century.
1646
AF
DF
The clothier's mark above the right-hand doorway containing the initials DF is that of Daniel Fowler who owned the house in the 17th century.
At one time clothiers' marks like these were used to identify who had produced each cloth offered for sale. The mark of a reputable clothier was a matter of pride and he might carve it on his mill or as here on his house. Sometimes it appears on his tombstone or brass memorial.

banners on the site for about nine years.

They manufactured gas engines and other heavy machinery. The directors were James Dickerson Humpidge, Henry Theodore Humpidge and Tom Graves-Smith. Their factory and office block alongside Selsley Hill were later to become home to Hampton Cars. Reference to the aerial photograph on Page 30 shows clearly the location of the Dudbridge Ironworks site and the variety of different buildings then in use, including those which are significant to our story.

The five storey building dominating the foreground is now known as Kimmins Mill and was originally built by Stanley Marling in 1849. It was J.C.C. Kimmins who later developed this most productive flour mill and by the 1890's was milling £50,000 worth of wheat per year. A special rail track to the 2nd floor was constructed to take flour directly to Dudbridge Station for speedy distribution. The 15 foot waterwheel was in use until about 1936 when production finally ceased. Interestingly, this long derelict mill has recently been restored as part of the re-development of the area and has become an imposing landmark again at what is now being called the new Gateway to Stroud.

The cottages on the left are the only other buildings remaining on the site and since 1894 the right hand cottage, "Riverside", has been the home of the Halliday family. The present owner, Miss Eileen Halliday, can remember the Hampton cars driving out of the works in the late Twenties. Her father, Gilbert, was a manager at the Ironworks.

The Dudbridge Ironworks Co. was employing 200 people in the early years of the twentieth century including well trained draughtsmen and designers and was utilising most of the site. They combined the old textile machinery business of Holborow with the heavy engineering expertise of Humpidge and developed an impressive range of gas engines up to 16 tons in weight.

continued on Page 31

Inside the Ironworks c.1914. Gilbert Halliday consults his notebook.

Miss Eileen Halliday

c1928

Unfortunately, when they were in full swing and exporting to many parts of the world, disaster struck. In June 1903, the managing director and leading light, James Humpidge and fitter, William French, were killed when a large flywheel disintegrated under test in the factory. Mr. Humpidge was acknowledged to be a brilliant engineer and at the time of his death was president of the Gloucestershire Engineering Society. The mourners at his funeral included John Fielding and Francis J. Platt, directors of the well known Gloucester engineering company bearing their name and where James Humpidge had been apprenticed. Despite this severe blow the Company continued and Mr. Platt purchased Humpidge's shares and joined the Board. However, it appears that prior to the war the demand for gas engines and related machines had been declining due to the rapid introduction of electricity and the business began to decline. For example, in 1914 on the other side of the road, Charles Apperly installed new electric power at his textile mill.

Before the outbreak of The Great War, the Company became sole concessionaires for the British Empire of Salmson aero engines.

During the war they were kept busy with the quality control, testing and warehousing of these interesting water cooled radial engines in association with Willans and Robinson of Rugby to whom they sub-contracted most of the manufacturing. One of these fine Canton-Unné System engines survives in the London Science Museum.

The Gloucestershire Industrial Archaeological Society (R.L. Rose) carried out a study of Dudbridge in 1966 and produced a fascinating account of the various activities and companies who have operated on this and nearby sites. Detailed repetition of this excellent work is far beyond the scope of our particular story. However, the concluding paragraphs of the report read as follows :

"One can walk from one end to the other in less than five minutes, or flash through it in a car without seeing a single item worth stopping for. Yet we have here engineering from the cast iron wheels of the millwright to aero engines and motor cars. We have cloth from the twelfth century fuller to the complexities of a twentieth century cloth mill. We have the rise and fall of brickmaking and

Salmson
AERO ENGINES
(CANTON-UNNE SYSTEM.)
Sole Concessionaires for the British Empire:
THE DUDBRIDGE IRON WORKS, LTD.,
STROUD,
GLOUCESTERSHIRE.

flour milling, the interplay of road, rail and canal transport; the elegance of an eighteenth century clothier's house and the grime of a modern foundry.

"I believe that the history of a site, such as Dudbridge, is a record of logical development; that every new phase depends on the conditions existing at the time, the geographic facts, the existing industries, the general economic outlook, the characters of the men who built and planned."

After the war, in February 1920, the directors sold their shares to Mr. J. Rowell and soon after Charles Apperly and Colonel Hugh Knothe became involved, along with Sir Percival Marling and William Selwyn. The Company staggered on making rubber processing plant and other equipment until it was placed into voluntary liquidation in 1926/7 after suffering heavy losses. Charles Apperly's losses in this operation in the early Twenties must have contributed to his eventual exit from car manufacturing and engineering in general.

In much later years, this site became home to many different businesses including Whitfield Engineering, Ballingers, Pye Transport, Red and White Services, Mitchell Cotts, Whitminster Grain Stores, Millvale Enterprises and latterly the foundry of Lewis & Hole.

SALMSON (CANTON-UNNÉ) 2M.7, 200hp/1,300rpm was a 14-cylinder, water-cooled, two-row radial poppet-valve engine. Bore/stroke 122 x 140mm Diameter 41.3 in

***Aircraft*:**

- Kennedy Giant
- Short Type A S.90 Admiralty Type 166
- Sopwith Bat Boat II
- Sopwith Special Seaplane, Admiralty Type C
- Sopwith Admiralty Type 860 Seaplane
- Wight A.I Navyplane.

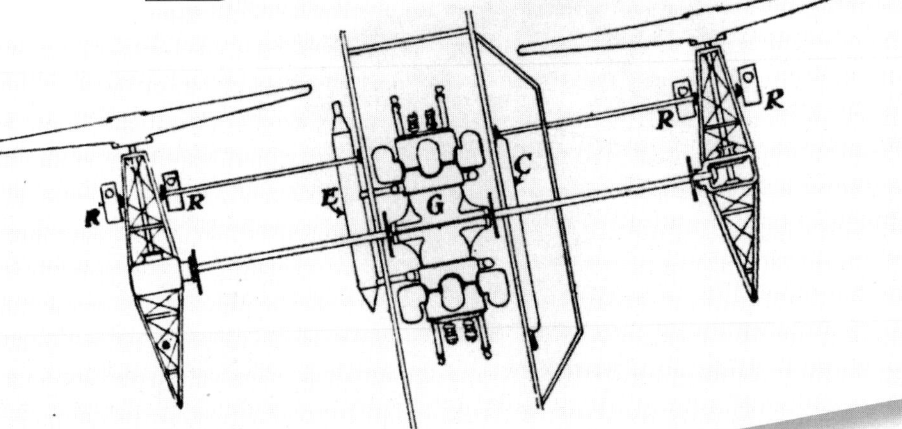

A plan of the 600hp Dudbridge Ironworks Salmson power unit, showing the arrangement of the transmission and the special nacelles for carrying twin propellers.
C : Oil reservoir. E : Silencer. G : Gearbox. R : Radiators.

A 2M.7 Salmson aero engine under test at the Dudbridge Works. The right hand figure is believed to be Arnold Levien, a French engineer from Salmson, Paris.

3
The Hampton comes to Gloucestershire

The original 1920 radiator badge.

Charles Apperly was certainly a motoring enthusiast - often seen at the wheel of a variety of vehicles before The Great War, though his father, Sir Alfred Apperly, employed his own chauffeur/mechanic. The Apperlys of Rodborough Court may well have been the first local family to transfer a distinctive registration plate from car to car.

Charles Apperly at the wheel of a Peugeot (AD 234) outside Dudbridge Mill (Apperly, Curtis). Sir Alfred, his father is seated in the rear. Charlie Allen is the recently elected MP. for Stroud - possibly 1910.

Their number, **AD 234**, was used on a 7hp Star, 20hp Climax, 16/20hp Argyle and two Peugeots of 18/20hp and 23/30hp. Unfortunately, no photographs of Charles driving a Hampton have yet come to light so we do not know if **AD 234** was ever seen on a Hampton model.

It now seems clear that his decision in 1914 to invest in the original Hampton company in Birmingham along with Wright and Radmore was motivated partly by his interest in motoring in general but more importantly by his desire to develop his component manufacturing business, The Stroud Metal & Plating Co. Ltd. He had rescued and re-formed this old established company in 1899 and by 1904 had erected new buildings and considerably broadened its manufacturing capability. This now included steam and water valves, gauges and many parts for the fast emerging electrical and motor trades, adding to its traditional business of umbrella fittings and brass castings. By 1919 they were employing around 300 people and ready to take advantage of the expected post war boom.

Was it always his intention to bring motor manufacturing to the Stroud area

Peugeot c1906 Chauffeur in attendance.

DUPLICATE FOR THE FILE.

No. 154769

Certificate of Incorporation

I Hereby Certify, That the
Hampton Engineering Company Limited

is this day Incorporated under the Companies Acts, 1908 to 1917, and that the Company is Limited.

Given under my hand at London this *First* day of *May* One Thousand Nine Hundred and *Nineteen*

Fees and Deed Stamps £ *3-10/-*

Stamp Duty on Capital £ *= 5/-*

Registrar of Joint Stock Companies.

Certificate received by *R Platt*

JORDAN & SONS, LIMITED REGISTRATION AGENTS 5 MAY 1919 CHANCERY LANE LONDON

Date

or was it the persuasive overtures of William Paddon towards the end of the war that brought about the move to Stroud and the building of a new factory close to Apperly, Curtis & Co. Ltd. - his existing textile mill and next door to his engineering company ? Whatever their motivation, the start-up was brisk with William Paddon, Harry Tremelling (an engine draughtsman from Hampshire) and several others being taken onto the payroll of The Stroud Metal & Plating Co. Ltd. in late 1918 in order to begin preparation for car production. At that stage, space and general facilities were limited but as Charles Apperly was Chairman of the host company he was obviously prepared to risk some disruption to his established business in the short term, until the new factory was ready for occupation.

The Hampton Engineering Co. Ltd. (No. 154769) was incorporated on 1st May 1919 and was granted permission to use the name of the old one which had been dissolved in December 1918. Initially, Charles Apperly and William Paddon held 1,000 one shilling (5p) ordinary shares each (i.e. Total £50 x 2 = £100). At the same time Charles' wife Florence was issued with 1,000 One Pound preferred ordinary shares - value £1,000.

Apperly and Paddon were the directors and Joseph Webber the company secretary. Paddon had not been a director or shareholder in the original Kings

"The Beeches" Thrupp.

William Paddon, creator of the Hampton.

Norton enterprise but it seems most likely that when the pre-war ascents of Nailsworth Ladder by the original Hampton cars were taking place, Apperly and Paddon became friends so this new alliance was logical. After all, Paddon had the motor engineering knowledge and Apperly had access to the capital and the desire to establish more engineering activities to halt the decline in his textile empire. The availability of skilled labour, materials and good road & rail communications must have given them additional confidence. Paddon quickly set about building a team to organise the construction of the new cars. Initially he lived at "The Little House", Rodborough Common, then moved to a charming house in Thrupp, on the fringes of Stroud, called "The Beeches".

In June 1919 two Extraordinary General Meetings were held with a view to re-structuring the capital of the company. Consequently, the authorised share capital was increased to £100,000 by the creation of 99,900 shares of One Pound each, divided into 50,000 cumulative preference shares (CPS) and 49,900 preferred ordinary shares (POS). The CPS holders would be entitled to a fixed dividend of 7.5% per annum and rank first in any winding up of the company. The POS holders would receive a 7.5% dividend "If and whenever the profits of the company will permit" plus a 2.5% bonus if surplus profits were made. This was later uplifted to 17.5% at an E.G.M. in October 1919. These holders would rank second in any winding up. The ordinary shareholders (Apperly and Paddon) would be entitled to anything left after the preference holders had been satisfied and would rank third in any winding up. The effect of the foregoing can be summarised as follows :

	£1 CPS	£1 POS	ORDINARY One Shilling (5p)
Apperly	12,500	13,500	1,000
Paddon	12,500	12,500	1,000
8 other investors including Joseph Webber	3,983	5,232	
Total	£28,983	£31,232	£100 (Previously subscribed)

The CPS and POS shares issued to Apperly and Paddon were allotted "for the purchase of goodwill, patterns and designs of The Hampton Engineering Company" - not for cash.

It is likely that Florence Apperly's preferred ordinary shares were passed to Charles in this re-structuring which explains why he now owned 1,000 more POS's than Paddon. At the same time an alteration was made to the Articles of Association which reveals that POS's now carried one vote for every 50 held so in the event of a conflict Apperly would have the upper hand.

Lloyds Bank, through their Capital and Counties Branch in Stroud did not appear to be offering much financial support at this stage but their cheque design for Hampton Cars was most attractive.

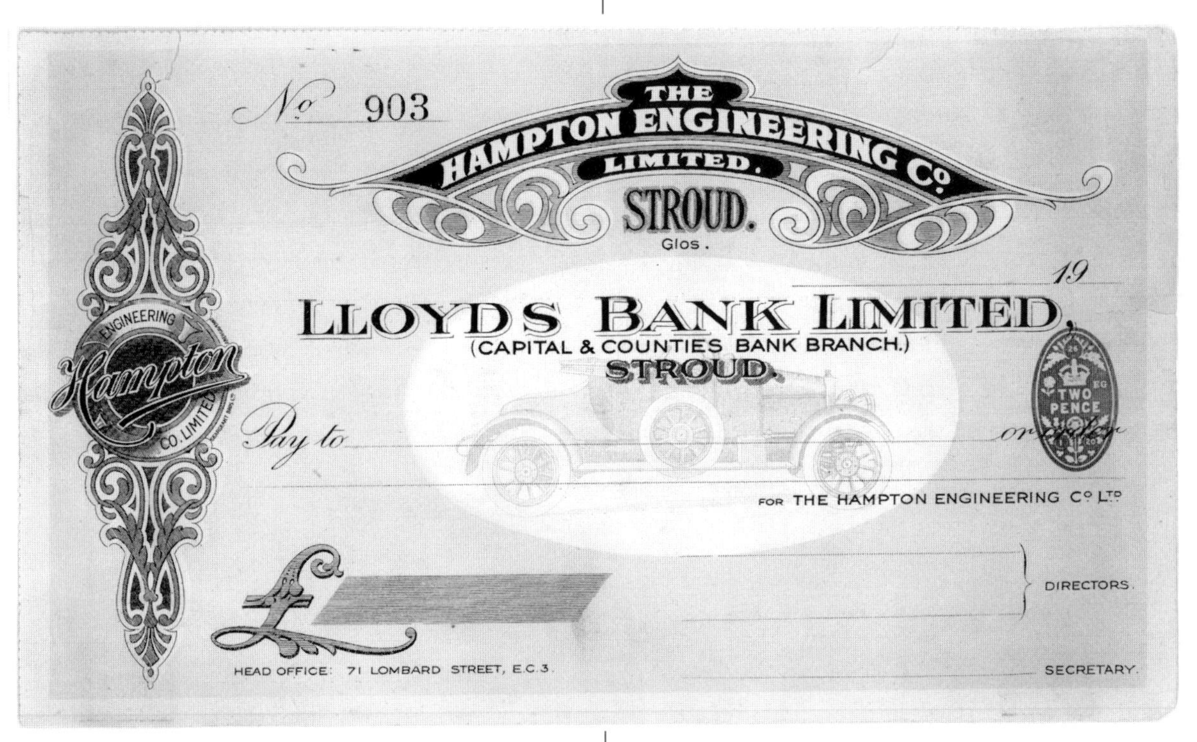
No 903

THE HAMPTON ENGINEERING Co LIMITED.
STROUD.
Glos.

19

LLOYDS BANK LIMITED,
(CAPITAL & COUNTIES BANK BRANCH.)
STROUD.

Pay to ________ or order

TWO PENCE

FOR THE HAMPTON ENGINEERING Co LTD

£

DIRECTORS.

HEAD OFFICE: 71 LOMBARD STREET, E.C.3.

SECRETARY.

Surprisingly, even before the Company became a legal entity the motoring Press was carrying details of the new Hampton 10 hp car in February 1919 with a 60mm x 120mm (1357cc) engine, side valve and of pre-war origin - perhaps a Chapuis-Dornier unit.

This was the post war pre-production prototype which as expected bore a strong resemblance to the 1914 model. The pre-war radiator had been changed; the "eye-brow" was more restrained than the design that was later adopted and it was also narrower and sloped backwards. The wheelbase measured 8 foot 6 inches and the track 4 foot. The price was expected to be £250 complete with Lucas lighting and two seater bodywork. The policy of stating a price even before the design or engine had been finalised seems rather naïve but Paddon saw this as a method of creating interest in his cars even though it would be around nine months before any production cars were available.

1919 - The prototype car.

Mr. Paddon was fortunate to locate and re-employ his former patternmaker from the Lifford Mill factory - Mr. Albert Moore, from Alum. Rock, Birmingham.

The differential case cover from Albert's pattern.

Albert Henry Moore (1878 - 1973)

Max Williamson was able to interview him in the fifties and his eye-witness observations are unique to our story because he is the only employee to work at the Kings Norton factory and at Dudbridge. He made all the wooden patterns for the iron and aluminium castings used in the car. These patterns were loaned out to various foundries who supplied the castings to the Company.

Max talks to Albert.

As Mr. Moore remembers it, assembly of the cars was carried out in the single main building which was quite small and still possessed the water wheel which had powered the mill in former times. He thinks the floor was merely earth - it was certainly very damp.

His pattern shop was in the converted residence of a former mill owner or manager and the only machinery was a hand-driven bandsaw and a treadle operated lathe. (Pictured in Chapter 1). The whole work force numbered less than two dozen, including one clerk who was the office "staff" and who utilised an old workman's cottage for his office.

Mr. Moore was on very good terms with Mr. Paddon but saw nothing of him during the War. He was very surprised therefore when one day in 1919 he saw an advertisement in a Birmingham newspaper asking him to get into touch. He did so and learned that Mr. Paddon was starting production of the Hampton in Stroud and invited him to join the Company - which he did. Mr. Moore's first task was to try and recover the patterns which had never been collected from the foundries. After some difficulty he collected most of them, in spite of the fact that some of the foundries had still not been paid for their pre-war work ! One pattern never recovered was the cover for the differential case of the back axle and Mr. Moore had to make a new one in a hurry. This cover bore the "Hampton" insignia and, for speed, Mr. Moore used the insignia from the radiator as a pattern. Comparison of the measurements of the insignia on the radiator of my car with that on the back axle confirms Mr. Moore's memory.

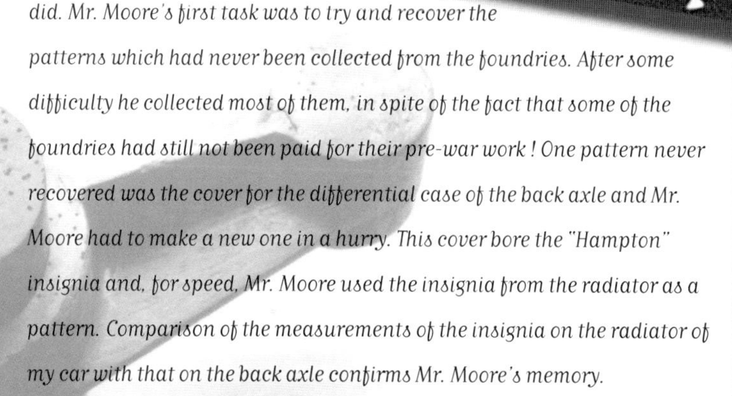

The only wooden pattern that survives measures $7^{1}/_{2}$" long.

Albert Moore's frank description of the Birmingham factory does not accord with the sales brochure of 1914 which is detailed in Chapter 1. Perhaps all sales brochures are inclined to romance a little ! Albert Moore actually joined in March 1919 as Foreman patternmaker. Henry Thomas Baxter (known as Harry) joined on 30th March 1920 as a trainee draughtsman and ultimately became their longest serving employee.

In the early days at Dudbridge, before the new factory on the north side of the Dudbridge Road was completed, space for assembly of complete cars in the old Ironworks premises was quite inadequate. Owing to the shortage of space the car bodies were subcontracted to Chalford Woodworks, adjacent to Belvedere Mill, the New Avon Body Company in Leamington Spa and AVRO of Manchester. Other adjacent properties were pressed into use including the Bidlake woollen mill.

Twelve original factory blueprints mounted on plywood (for shop floor use) were discovered several years ago hidden away in one of the old workshops. Although they have deteriorated it is possible to make out several components including hood sticks, brake parts, special nuts, washers, ignition levers, tubes and other components dated from 1922 to 1924. The only drawing from 1919 is that of a 10hp brake and clutch pedal pad depicting its "H" monogram.

Despite the many difficulties the

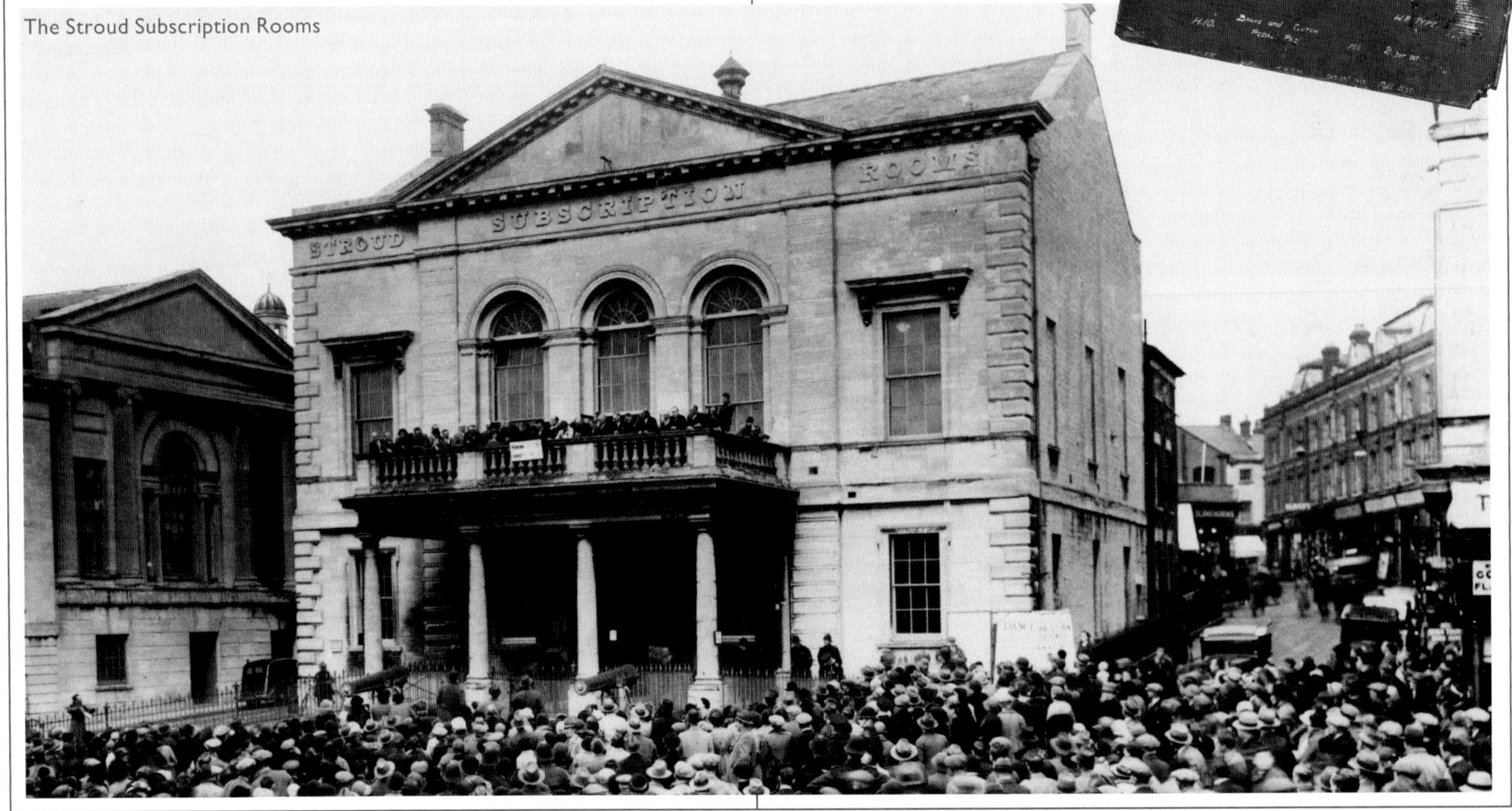

The Stroud Subscription Rooms

continued on Page 46

The Hampton Car de Luxe.

Fitted with Lucas or Brolt Dynamo Lighting and Starting Set, Klaxon, Dunlop Tyres and Tyre on Spare Wheel.

~~**Price £495 net, complete.**~~

Price £520 net, complete.

The 1920 sales brochure with over-printed price increase.

FOREWORD

In presenting our **Catalogue,** we feel that no explanation of our policy is necessary beyond the fact that we realise the growing demand, both at home and overseas, for a reliable high grade car at a price commensurate with the material and workmanship employed in its construction.

It is the quiet, but steady and increasing testimony of thoroughly contented owners, relying on **Hampton Cars** every day for business or touring work, in all climates, under every condition of road service, that is responsible, more than any other factor, for the remarkable position which this car has gained in the markets of the world.

The "**Hampton Car**" described herein is an attempt to give the purchasing public better value than has ever been possible before, and we believe from the measure of success which has attended our efforts in this direction, that we have succeeded in calling attention to the fact, that it is still possible to produce a British built car at a price comparing favourably with the imported production of foreign factories; and which, as regards quality, design, workmanship, and finish, leaves nothing to be desired. Designed and constructed by engineers who have gained their experience in the leading British factories; embodying in its construction all that is best, both as regards design and material; assembled by skilled mechanics, under the direct and personal supervision of a responsible management—the specification of the "**Hampton**" **Car** outlined in these pages is well worth your earnest consideration.

We shall be most pleased at any time to send a car for your trial and inspection without placing you under any obligation to purchase.

Should there be any point upon which you would like further information, our technical correspondence department is always at your service, and assuring you of our best attention at all times, we beg to remain,

Yours very faithfully,

The Hampton Engineering Co. Ltd.

STROUD, GLOS.,
ENGLAND.

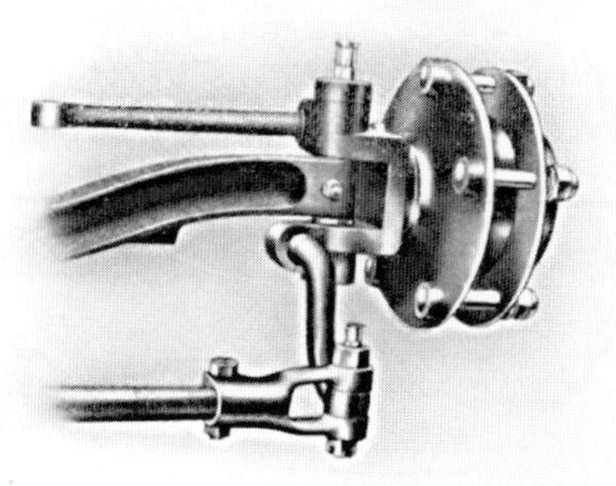

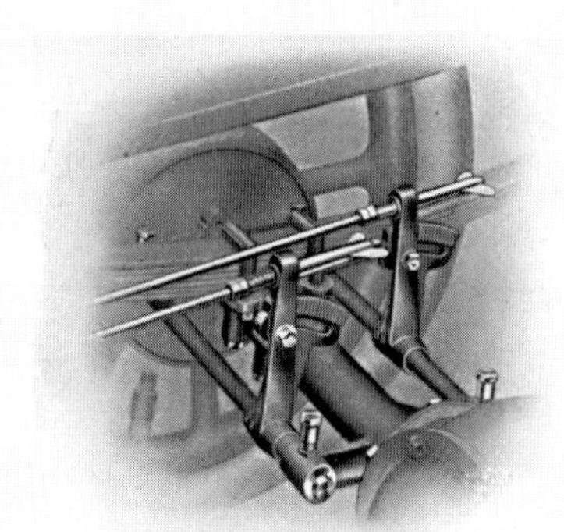

The Hampton Car, 10/16 h.p.

SPECIFICATION.

Chassis. Frame of pressed steel. Wheelbase 9′0″. Front springs half elliptic, rear three-quarter elliptic, very long. All shackle pins and eye bolts fitted with screw down grease lubricators.

Engine. 10/16 h.p. Four cylinders cast en bloc, 63 × 120. Enclosed overhead valves. Adjustable tappets. Detachable head.

Cooling. Thermo-syphon with radiator and impeller in water jacket of engine. Special allowance made for hot climates.

Lubricating. Forced feed and trough lubrication to every engine bearing, by pump in sump. Indicator on dash.

Carburetter. Zenith or Claudel automatic. Vertical type.

Magneto. Watford high tension. Watertight enclosed type.

Clutch. Leather to metal, extremely light.

Gear Box. Three speeds and reverse. Ball bearings throughout. Gate change.

Universal Joints. Special Hampton design, require no lubrication.

Transmission. Bevel drive, specially strong, mounted on ball bearings with ball thrusts. The wheels are mounted on outer sleeves, so that the differential shafts carry no weight. Specially high clearance for rough roads.

Brakes. Foot and side brakes, internal expanding, enclosed in dust proof drums, both acting on the rear wheels Thus no brake strain comes on transmission.

Steering Worm and sector, irreversible.

Control. By accelerator pedal.

Front Axle. Of H section steel, very strong; Caster type steering swivels, mounted on long bearings, making steering extremely light to handle.

Wheels. 710 × 90, Sankey steel, interchangeable and detachable; spare wheel.

Tyres. Five 710 × 90, Dunlop. Grooved.

Starting and Lighting. Lucas, Brolt, or other approved electric lighting and starting equipment.

Klaxon warning signal.

The Hampton Engineering Co. Ltd., reserve the right to modify this Specification, or any part of it, without notice.

Chassis Price **£395** net, delivered at works.

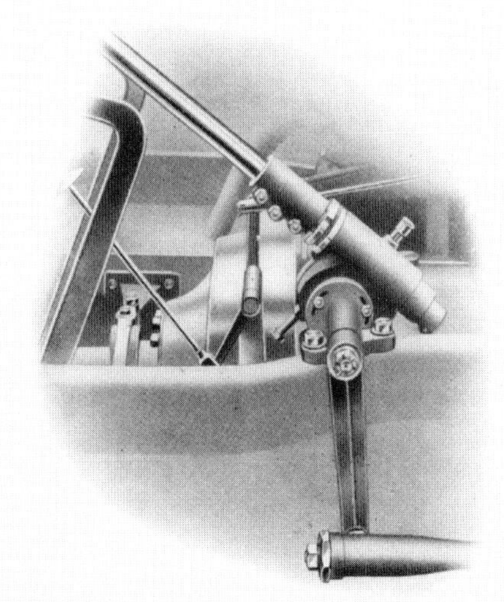

ENGINE

10/16 h.p. (1496 cc's), 63 m/m bore by 120 m/m stroke; aluminium bloc casting; cast-iron cylinder liners; all valves in head of special alloy steel, large diameter, interchangeable; the design following aero engine practice throughout, and making for a remarkably efficient engine. The cylinder heads are readily detachable, without dismantling the whole engine, for the purpose of examination and decarbonising when required. Valve push rods are adjustable, and valve rockers are entirely enclosed in an aluminium cover plate, the fulcrum pins being lubricated by an entirely new method, ensuring absence of wear and complete silence.

The main bearings are of large area, babitted with a special alloy, and fed with oil under pressure from force pump in crank chamber sump, the connecting rod ends dipping in constant level troughs, the whole lubricating system being so regulated that the amount of oil is directly proportional to the work being done by the engine, any excess escaping through a pressure relief valve—**thus ensuring perfect and continuous lubrication, and a smokeless exhaust.**

IGNITION

High Tension British-made Watford Magneto, water-tight enclosed type.

COOLING

Thermo-Syphon cooling by means of special Hampton honeycomb radiator and impeller situated in front of engine block.

CARBURETTER

Latest type Zenith horizontal automatic; gives about 30 miles to the gallon of petrol and operates equally well with benzole without any adjustment, the mileage and power then showing an increase, a point worth your serious consideration.

An oil pressure gauge is fitted on the dashboard in front of driver, and a "dipper" tell-tale on the engine sump at once indicates the necessity or otherwise of renewing the supply. The water jacketing of the engine is particularly efficient, the cooling of the cylinder heads and valve ports having received special attention—overheating is unknown on Hampton cars. **Electric Self Starter** is fitted as part of standard equipment, and the engine is mounted on special brackets, giving three point suspension and absolute immunity from torsional strain due to bad road surfaces.

The power curve of the high efficiency engine, fitted in Hampton Cars, is to all intents and purposes a straight line, and at 2,000 revs. per minute, the average engine develops 20 B.H.P. —approximating 1 h.p. per 100 revs.—which is some measure of the general efficiency of the whole design.

HAMPTON—"THE HILL CLIMBER.'

OVERSEA ORDERS.

The Hampton Engineering Co., Ltd., give exceptional attention to Overseas orders. Appreciating the necessity for gaining the confidence of their clients abroad, the management endeavour to personally superintend the details connected with such shipment. Economy of crating and freighting is not lost sight of, and the cheapest and best route for transit is selected if such matters are left to them.

THE TERMS OF BUSINESS for all such orders are one-third with order and the balance on delivery to clients' packers.

COST OF PACKING AND FREIGHT.

The approximate cost of packing a Hampton chassis is about £17 10s. 0d., and a complete car about £18 10s. 0d., depending on the measurements, and includes all cartage charges in London and delivery as far now as Royal Albert Docks on the Thames.

Overseas clients will greatly facilitate business by instructing their own local bankers to pay us the deposit and balance. This may be done by Cable, if urgent, followed by written instructions.

APPROXIMATE COST OF FREIGHT (including packing and supplying Waterproof Cases) to various parts of the world of Hampton Chassis. *(Liable to variation without notice.)*

GOODS.	FROM	TO	RATE.
Hampton Chassis in cases not exceeding 12ft. 4in. × 5ft. × 4ft. 6in. Nett weight 11 cwts. each. At Owners risk.	Port of London. Collected from rail, including supply of case and packing with waterproof paper lining.	Cape Town, Algoa Bay	£47 0 0
		East London, Natal	48 15 0
		Delagoa Bay	51 0 0
		Callao	68 0 0
		Valparaiso	66 10 0
		Penang, Singapore	47 15 0
		Hong Kong	48 15 0
		Auckland, Wellington, Lyttleton, Port Chalmers ...	56 10 0
		Adelaide, Melbourne, Sydney	55 0 0
		Bombay, Calcutta, Madras, Karachi, Colombo ...	43 5 0

Cars complete requiring larger packing cases and more space than Chassis cost approximately 15% to 20% extra on the above rates. Rates may vary at any time. Carriage on Cars or Chassis to packers and port of shipment is in all cases borne by purchaser.

A 1922 12hp Chalford semi-sporting 2 seater meets a pre-war relative outside the Dudbridge factory.

BC 6083 is a 1914 - 4 seater tourer torpedo built at Lifford Mill.

company organised a large dinner in October 1919 which was reported in detail in The Stroud Journal on 14th November. "200 employees dinner at Subscription Rooms." Whilst Hamptons probably had less than 50 employees at this early stage, the remainder of those attending would have been from The Stroud Metal & Plating Co. Ltd. together with friends and guests.

Excerpts from the report of this morale boosting occasion read as follows : The Chairman, Charles Apperly, in his address appealed for "continuation of unity of purpose between management and workers in a period of strikes and unrest" amongst other things. He then called upon Mr. Paddon to speak. Paddon said "they would be pleased to know that on the first day of the Olympia Motor Show they had 15,000 people on the Hampton stand." (Applause). It seemed incredible. They had made in seven months a motor car which was the centre of attraction of the buying markets of the world. They had come from India, Africa, Ceylon, all the British colonies without exception, Holland, Sweden, Norway, Denmark. They had done the seemingly impossible and in seven months they had produced a chassis where other firms with bigger works and better facilities had not been able to exhibit because they had not been able to produce the goods. They would be glad to hear that they had Royalty on the Hampton stand. Before he left the Show he had himself taken orders for over 400 Hampton chassis (loud applause). It was the workers who had done this and as long as they worked with and not against the management, the directors would help them. As long as they worked together, success was certain (hear, hear). Their polished chassis on which they had worked so hard was on show and was admired by everyone.

An illustrated 3 colour brochure was issued early in 1920 parts of which are reproduced. Careful comparison with the 1914 publication indicates remarkable similarities with just a few words altered here and there - both obviously the work of Paddon.

An interesting word variation relates to the gearbox : 1914 - copy concludes with "The whole has been designed with a very wide margin of strength and may be safely entrusted to the worst type of driver." 1920 says "to the most indifferent driver." Perhaps Paddon should have concentrated on the engineering and left the copy-writing to someone else but in a small organisation he probably had no alternative ! Dealers were not listed in this early brochure and two blank pages were designated "Coupé and Specification" and "Four Seater Hampton" - "blocks in course of preparation".

On the surface it would appear that things at Hampton Cars were developing in a satisfactory manner with a full order book, a new Works being built with some of the new capital injected in June, a settled labour force and an attractive product for which there was a good demand.

In reality, however, as early as January 1920 Charles Apperly was desperately trying to reconstruct the Company yet again and at an E.G.M. on the 19th January the following resolutions were passed:

A. "That in order to provide for the necessary extension of the Company's business it is desirable to reconstruct the Company and accordingly that the Company be wound-up voluntarily and that Joseph James Webber of Dudbridge Mills, Stroud, be and he is hereby appointed Liquidator for the purpose of such winding-up.

B. "That the said Liquidator be and he is hereby authorised to consent to the registration of a new Company to be named The Hampton Engineering Company Limited." From the Official Receiver's Report, it later transpired that "The Company went into liquidation for the purpose of amalgamation with The Stroud Metal Company Limited and it was the intention that the undertaking and assets of both Companies should be sold and transferred to a third Company which was to be formed" presumably keeping the name of Hampton Engineering Co. Ltd.

The catalogue contains several references to "Hampton - the Hill Climber" See Chapter 5.

"The said Liquidator carried on the business of the Company with a view to the beneficial winding-up thereof and in the hope of carrying through the proposed amalgamation until the month of October 1920. The negotiations between the two Companies were of a very protracted and difficult nature; the financial position of the Company became embarrassed while many trade creditors were pressing their claims and eventually the scheme of amalgamation was found to be impracticable."

By 17th September 1920 new joint Liquidators (Messrs. Appleby & Brooke-Hitching) had been appointed in place of poor old Joseph Webber who was probably out of his depth in trying to achieve the near impossible task of carrying through an ill-conceived amalgamation. Webber was the company secretary of Stroud Metal and afterwards retained that position. The Apperly textile operation had been badly hit by the war and the loss-making Dudbridge Ironworks was making things worse. Clearly, he did not fully understand the capital hungry requirements of the emerging motor industry and certainly could not contribute directly to the engineering side of the business.

Apperly, Curtis Co. Ltd. retained ownership of the new factory and this was therefore not in the Liquidator's hands.

By November, car production was virtually at a standstill, owing to the inability to pay for engines and other services. It is hard to imagine that just one year after that euphoric dinner at the Subscription Rooms, Hampton Cars was broke and about to go out of business.

But a 21 year old customer from South Wales happened to call at the factory to buy a spare part and he was told about the sorry state of affairs at Hampton Cars. His name was Myrddin Daniel and as a satisfied owner and motoring enthusiast he went back to Wales and suggested to his wealthy father that here was a good opportunity to buy a motor manufacturer. John Daniel (knighted shortly afterwards) was a very successful businessman and indications are that he was keen to provide a suitable business opportunity for Myrddin. So the assets were purchased from the Liquidator for £10,000 and on Christmas Eve 1920 Hampton Engineering Company (1920) Ltd., Number 172256, was incorporated. This proved to be a welcome Christmas present for most of the loyal Hampton workers but sadly and surprisingly the car's creator, William Paddon, was excluded from the deal. In fact, his departure was a condition of the take-over. Albert Moore the patternmaker was also "not required".

Following the sale of the company, the Liquidators found themselves involved in several legal battles in 1921 regarding unsatisfactory payments to certain creditors including The Dunlop Rubber Co. Ltd., Cooper-Steward Engineering Co. Ltd. and closer to home, Frederick Steel & Co. Ltd. of Ebley who printed Hampton's brochures. The adverse publicity resulting from these events would continue to be troublesome for the new Hampton company which still needed supplies and support, particularly from Dunlop. It was not until September 1924 that the original Dudbridge company was finally wound up. In all 245 cars were constructed during this formative period. Bearing in mind

This Hampton was supplied as a bare chassis in 1920. The owner, J.G. Gore, stripped the Dorman 9.8hp engine and balanced the reciprocating components which resulted in a top speed of over 60mph. The body with its nicely proportioned wings but still without a driver's door was made in Doncaster.

the factory was not finished when they started and they could not derive any benefits from the spring-board effect of war time production, this was a considerable achievement. However, the policy of building cars regardless of cost and without any clearly defined financial control almost brought The Stroud Metal Co. to its knees so the fact that the amalgamation did not take place was one of Charles Apperly's better financial decisions. It has been rumoured in the Stroud valleys that the drain on his financial resources caused by the Hampton Cars venture was a contributory factor to the eventual demise of his textile mill some ten years later in 1931.

William Paddon stayed in the Stroud area for a while and formed an alliance with a small Birmingham manufacturer - Autocrat Cars Ltd., who made a similar car to the Hampton complete with Dorman Engines - he even sent a most elaborate Christmas greetings card to some of his old workers 12 months later.

Fortunately, Max's Hampton (HT 1526) still survives from this period and its history and features are examined in Chapter 8.

1921-22.

With the Season's Greetings *W.P.*

"IN all human affairs there are *efforts;* and there are *results,* and the strength ... the measure of the

DECEMBER, 1921.

With the Season's Greetings and all Good Wishes for a Prosperous New Year to my many friends who, by their moral and material assistance in the past, have helped to make business mutually agreeable; and to whose support I confidently look forward in the future.

I am convinced that the ultimate car for the majority of users in the British Isles, will not exceed twelve horse-power under R.A.C. Rating, and will—apart from any question of sentiment—be of British manufacture throughout.

The hill has yet to be discovered that the average Light Car cannot climb—there are no roads it cannot travel on—nor has the limit of its speed been determined.

Every British built car you buy, means employment in one form or another for hundreds of your fellow countrymen.

STROUD,
GLOS.

EMPIRE HOUSE,
PICCADILLY,
LONDON, W.

Extracts from William Paddon's Christmas card

4
The Welsh era - Sir John takes over

NY 680 was supplied in chassis form to the Berw Carriage Works, Pontypridd, Wales.

Sir John Daniel was born in Carmarthen in 1870 and in the company's Official Register his occupation was given as "miller". At that time he was chairman of The Avana Milling Company of Cardiff and Port Talbot and had financial interests in steel, shipping and coal mining in South Wales.

He was involved with local government, a keen vegetarian, a golfer and greatly interested in preservation of the Welsh tongue - perhaps that is why his only son was christened Myrddin although most contemporary observers, including Max Williamson, referred to him as Mervyn.

Initially, his Board of Directors at Hamptons comprised his son Myrddin, David T. Jones and himself as chairman, although in February Albert Bown (Motor Engineer), John Thomas (Outfitter) and William Renoden (Confectioner) became directors and investors. James Morgan was company secretary and accountant.

Bringing David T. Jones into the business was a wise move as he was a mature and experienced motor dealer who was running a large and successful retail company then known as The Neath and District Automobile & Posting Co. Ltd. which had been selling a few Hamptons manufactured by the previous management.

During an interview in the Sixties Myrddin claimed he was managing director but it appears that Jones played the major role due to his much greater experience; certainly by 1923 Jones was known to the Press as managing

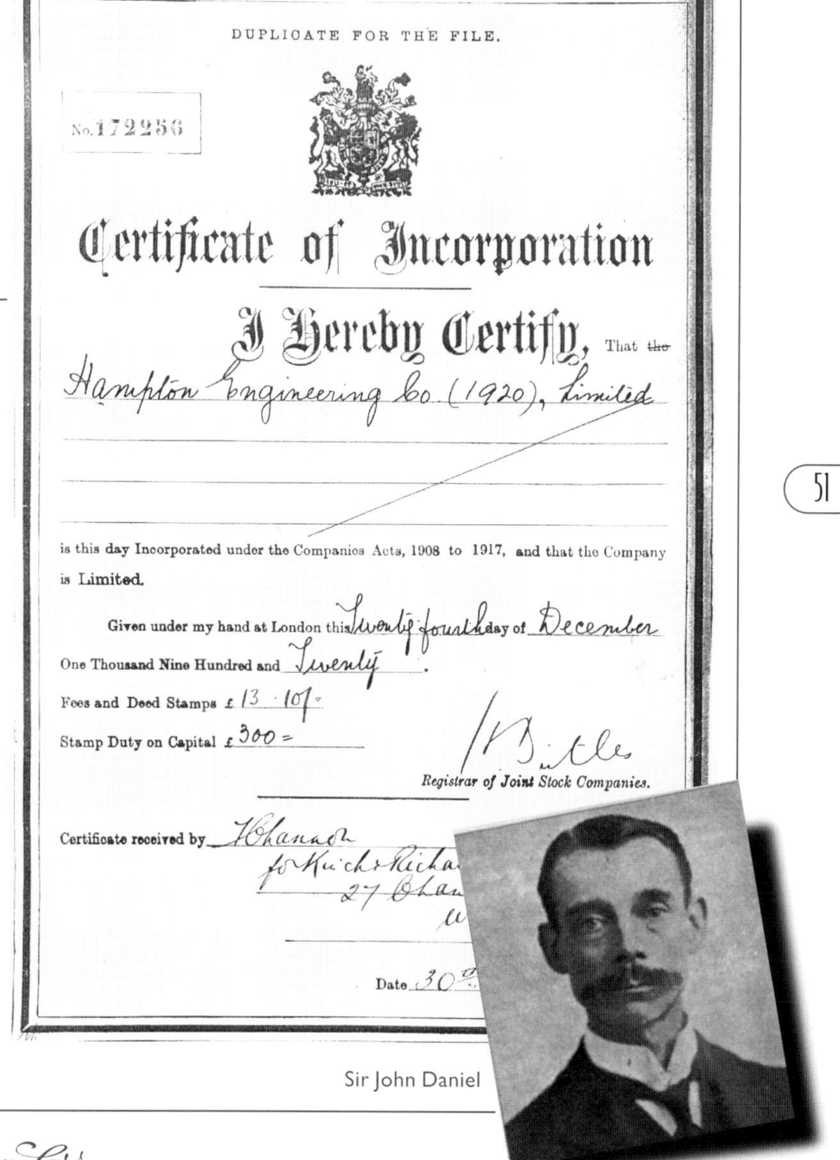

DUPLICATE FOR THE FILE.

No. 172256

Certificate of Incorporation

I Hereby Certify, That Hampton Engineering Co (1920), Limited

is this day Incorporated under the Companies Acts, 1908 to 1917, and that the Company is Limited.

Given under my hand at London this Twenty fourth day of December One Thousand Nine Hundred and Twenty.

Fees and Deed Stamps £ 13 · 10/-

Stamp Duty on Capital £ 300 =

Registrar of Joint Stock Companies.

Certificate received by

Date 30

Sir John Daniel

David T. Jones

director. The correct interpretation of this situation is probably that Myrddin, being the only full time director at the works, was managing the company as far as day to day matters were concerned, despite his tender years and lack of experience. Fortunately, for Myrddin and the company, Thomas P. Joseph was quickly recruited as chief designer/works engineer to replace Paddon. He came with a good pedigree having worked in senior positions with Rolls-Royce and Napier.

Telephone No. 81. Telegrams "Automobile."

17-22, ALFRED STREET,
NEATH, 192

The Neath and District Automobile Co., Ltd.

MANAGER - - MR. DAVID T. JONES.

AGENCIES.
Napier
Dennis
Crossley
Austin
Singer

AGENCIES.
Morris Cowley
Morris Oxford
Hampton
Buick
Chevrolet

It seems that Sir John was prepared to be more than just a figurehead in the company. He hosted a luncheon at the Holborn Restaurant in London in early January 1921 to promote his new business. He went out of his way to stress that "his company was entirely a new one and not in any sense a reconstruction of the old one." Strong words indeed and not really true. However, he went on to outline various improvements and obviously take the credit for them. Bearing in mind Paddon could only have left a few weeks beforehand, most of these "improvements" must have been in the pipeline and only held up by the autumn liquidation. Notwithstanding this the 1921 cars would have :

a) Zenith carburettors

b) Rear mounted fuel tank and auto-vac fuel feed (12hp only)

c) Hand controls for carburettor and magneto

d) Alteration of ratio of 2nd gear

e) Electric starting and lighting now fitted as standard.

Thomas P. Joseph.

He further announced that the old system of customer deposits would be abolished and that appointed agents would agree to carry stock so that at least one car would always be available for inspection by intending purchasers. He went on to announce his prices : "As regards price, the chassis will retail at £425 which (compared with the price of others of a similar power and grade) appears to be very reasonable. As to complete cars, the prices are as follows : open two-seater £565; open four-seater £596; two-seater coupé £650 and saloon £675. The sporting two-seater with specially long bonnet and only a single dickey-seat retails at the same price as the standard two-seater, namely £565." The post war boom was beginning to evaporate by 1921 and the Hampton pricing structure was symptomatic of the severe competition it was facing. Several sales brochures appeared in quick succession, one of which is illustrated. These revealed either over-printed lower figures or progressively cheaper prices. For example, the 4 seater tourer with 12hp Dorman engine is first listed at £596 in February 1921, then £550 in June, then £525 in August followed by a dramatic reduction to £395 at the end of the year. The smaller 10hp Hampton Junior two seater had slumped to £275 by the same time. Meanwhile, private owners continued to enter their cars in competitive motor sport events all over the country including the well publicised Nailsworth Ladder Hill Climb - just 4 miles from the works.

The dealer network was gradually extended to cover the whole country led by B.S. Marshall Ltd. of Hanover Square, London who became the backbone of their sales effort in the London area for several years. The enterprising owner, Bertie Marshall, and his racing Hampton are featured in

Page 6.

Extract from Registration Particulars.

(a) Mark and Number NY-680

(b) Type of Body 3 Seater & Double Dicky

(c) Colour Grey & Black

(d) Propulsion I.C.E.

(e) MANUFACTURER'S:—

Name Hampton

Description of Car 3 Seater & Double Dicky

Chassis Type Letter & No. 4 K. N.O.

No. of Engine 12909

(f) Year of Engine 1921

(g) INTERNAL COMBUSTION ENGINE:—

Cylinders with Single Piston 4

Cylinders with Two Pistons

Internal Diameter of Cylinders 69 m/m

... Books (Registration) have been handed over.

The Hampton car N.Y. 680 has been broken up and will not again be used on the road. The Registration Book in respect of this vehicle is surrendered.

Yours faithfully,

Imperial Motor Co.

Howell M Daniel

AND INITIALS OF ISSUING OFFICER.

John C. Morris took delivery in January 1922 pictured at beginning of this Chapter. Eleven years later, John sold it to the Imperial Motor Co. of Abercynon who scrapped it in October 1934 - effectively a "one owner" Hampton.

THE WONDER CAR OF 1923.

9-21 h.p., Overhead Valves, Self-starter, 4-speed Gearbox. Right Hand Control. Enots Grease System. Double Windscreen.

12 MONTHS' GUARANTEE.

PRICES:

2-seater Double Dickey £295
Chummy 4-seater... £325
Coupe Double Dickey £350

London Agents: B. S. MARSHALL LTD., 17a, Hanover Square.

HAMPTON Engineering Co. (1920), Ltd., Stroud—Glos.

'Phone: STROUD 271-272. Grams: "WIDAWAK, Stroud."

the next chapter. Closer to home, the Wicliffe Motor Company handled the local distribution from their Russell Street, Stroud showroom. A little later these dealers were issued with smart new vitreous enamel advertising plaques proclaiming" The superlative car" - a phrase later used in Hampton's advertising. It was the company's policy to support the annual White City/Olympia Motor Shows with a particularly impressive range of cars and engines being shown in October 1922.

To support their sales effort further Thomas Joseph was always interested in contributing to current motoring topics. Co-operating with The Motor magazine in the following road test was an interesting and typical example of this policy. The circumstances of this event have been summarised and the results given in full.

INSTRUCTIVE THREE AND FOUR SPEED GEAR TESTS - NEW LIGHT ON AN OLD CONTROVERSY.

In the early 1920's motor car designers had yet to form a consistent view as to the relative merits of three and four speed gearboxes. In order to examine the case, The Motor in conjunction with Hampton Cars conducted a test in October 1922, using a 12hp Meadows engined Hampton under controlled conditions.

The car with 3 passengers aboard was twice driven round a 35 mile route, the first time fitted with a four speed box, the second time with a three speed. The course started at the Hampton works in Dudbridge, climbed up the Cotswold escarpment via the famous Birdlip Hill, thence to Cirencester and back to Stroud on the main road. On each circuit the time up Birdlip Hill was noted, together with average speed, petrol consumption and the number of gear changes made. The test results are tabulated on the next page showing

the four speed box generally ahead. But perhaps the most surprising observation in today's terms is the extraordinarily low number of gear changes recorded on the three speed test - no doubt confirming that the roads were almost deserted at this time.

RESULTS OF THE TESTS AT A GLANCE.

THREE-SPEED BOX.

Ratios 4, 7.95, 15 to 1 forward; 19.8 to 1 reverse.

Number of up-and-down changes:—

First to second	1
Second to third	3
Third to second	2
Second to first	0
Total	=6

Time up Birdlip Hill, 4 mins. 23 secs.
Distance covered in one hour, 27.3 miles.

FOUR-SPEED BOX.

Ratios 4, 6.44, 9.28 and 15.39 to 1 forward; 21 to 1 reverse.

Number of up-and-down changes:—

First to second	1
Second to third	3
Third to fourth	4
Fourth to third	3
Third to second	2
Second to first	0
Total	=13

Time up Birdlip Hill, 3 mins. 55 secs.
Distance covered in one hour, 28.7 miles.

Petrol consumption.—An improvement of 6.4 miles per gallon was noted with the four-speed box. Maximum speed attained, about 50 m.p.h. Weight of car, 23 cwt. Tyre sizes, 710 mm. by 90 mm.

In common with other companies, Hamptons experienced power supply problems caused by the coal strikes in May 1921. Their resourceful management quickly overcame this problem by installing a heavy Leyland lorry in the Works which via a belting system from the rear wheels drove the overhead shafting to power their machines.

Max was fortunate to be able to interview Myrddin Daniel about his career at Hamptons and his verbatim report follows : Max talks to Myrddin

"At the time Sir John took over, the new factory was in use but uncompleted. Built by Monks of Bristol, it was of modern design and had an

Leyland lorry providing power to Hampton's Machine Shop,

26-2-21

Note the guarantee in the advertisement above and also the price of the four seater car. In the lower advertisement the price of a similar model is down by £46 - £70. One wonders how many buyers claimed refunds and if they got them.

18-6-21

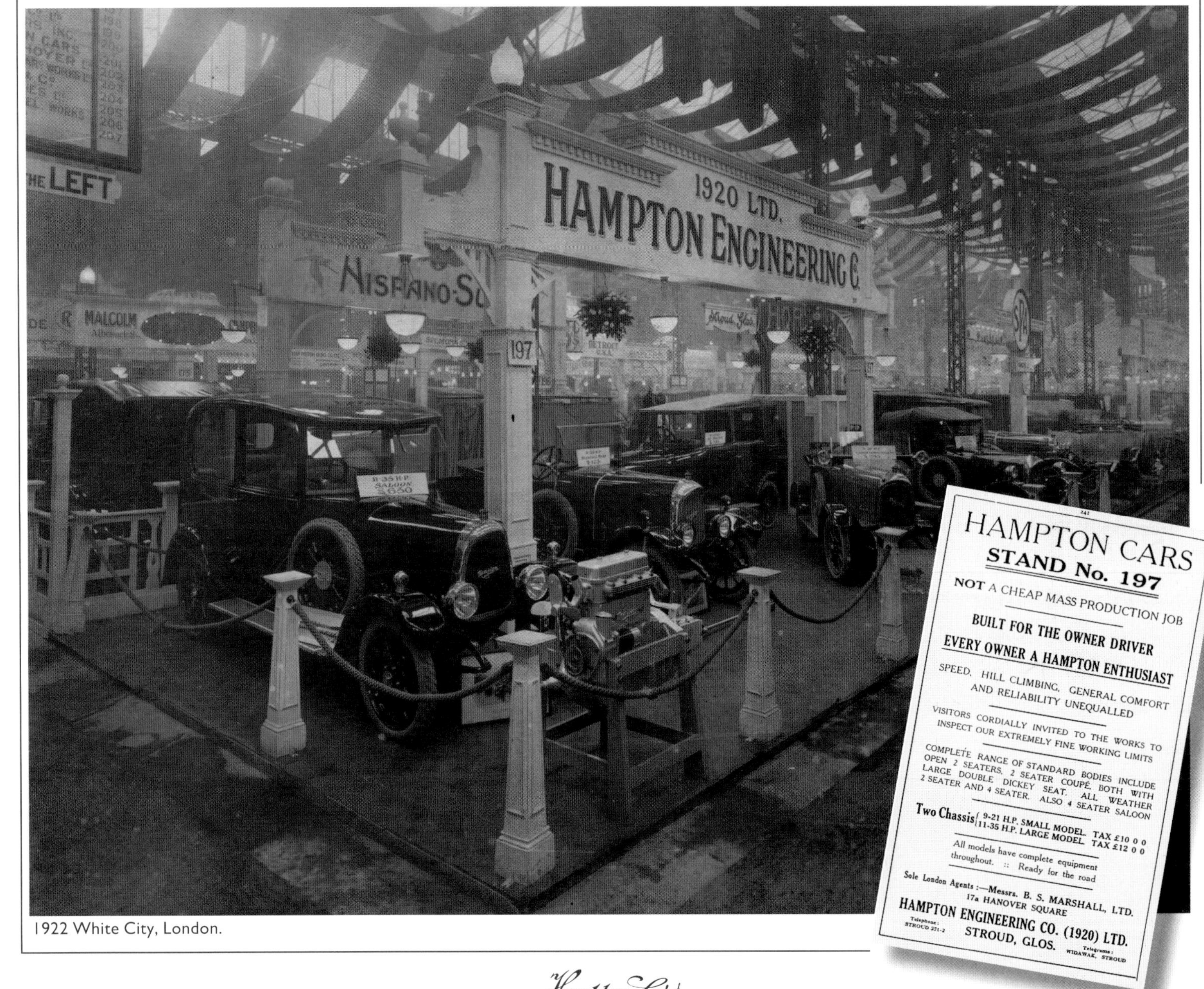

THE LEFT
1920 LTD.
HAMPTON ENGINEERING Co
HISPANO-SU
MALCOLM
197
HAMPTON CARS
STAND No. 197
NOT A CHEAP MASS PRODUCTION JOB
BUILT FOR THE OWNER DRIVER
EVERY OWNER A HAMPTON ENTHUSIAST
SPEED, HILL CLIMBING, GENERAL COMFORT AND RELIABILITY UNEQUALLED
VISITORS CORDIALLY INVITED TO THE WORKS TO INSPECT OUR EXTREMELY FINE WORKING LIMITS
COMPLETE RANGE OF STANDARD BODIES INCLUDE OPEN 2 SEATERS, 2 SEATER COUPÉ, BOTH WITH LARGE DOUBLE DICKEY SEAT. ALL WEATHER 2 SEATER AND 4 SEATER. ALSO 4 SEATER SALOON
Two Chassis { 9-21 H.P. SMALL MODEL. TAX £10 0 0
11-35 H.P. LARGE MODEL. TAX £12 0 0
All models have complete equipment throughout. :: Ready for the road
Sole London Agents :—Messrs. B. S. MARSHALL, LTD.
17a HANOVER SQUARE
HAMPTON ENGINEERING CO. (1920) LTD.
Telephone: STROUD 271-2
STROUD, GLOS.
Telegrams: WIDAWAK, STROUD

1922 White City, London.

Painting & Trimming

unsupported roof span of 100 feet - very unusual at that time. Many architects and other visitors came to see the factory.

"Mr. Daniel confirmed to me that Hamptons made almost every part of the car themselves, except for the engine, the chassis frames from Rubery Owen and rough forgings for the front axle from Vickers. Thanks to Mr. Paddon's passion for the very best in machinery, the factory was exceptionally well equipped. Spiral bevels for the back axle were cut on American Gleason machines. Some bodywork was made by Hamptons and some by Avon of Leamington. Some customers bought chassis and had bodywork specially made for them. Two seaters with a curved-in back were of Hampton manufacture and flush-sided ones were Avon products. The normal method of finishing cars at that time was by coach paint applied by brush. The long drying period between coats meant that a high quality body took weeks to complete and a very large amount of capital was tied up in partly

The Workforce

completed bodies. Hamptons had a special heated drying room in one corner of the body shop and the drying period was cut to 4 or 5 hours. Mr. Daniel told me how, on one occasion, he put this drying room to good use. One morning he had a brush with the police and thought they had taken the details of his car. He dashed back to the Works, had the red car painted black and put in the drying room. As soon as it was dry he took it out and got it thoroughly muddy. When the police came to the Works with details of a red Hampton, number so-and-so, it was pointed out that the only car of that number was black. They retired baffled ! It should be pointed out that Mr. Daniel was only 21 at this time and, he admits, not as responsible as he later became with maturity.

Myrddin Daniel at the wheel.

The original Dudbridge Works & Offices

"Dunlop tyres were normally fitted but Hamptons were given a supply of some newly-imported American Partridge tyres to test. They were excellent and B.S. Marshal tried them out at Brooklands on the racing Hampton with highly satisfactory results. A contract was signed and all Hamptons were to be fitted with Partridge tyres. However, when the production tyres arrived they turned out to be useless. For several days the telephone was constantly ringing with irate customers complaining that the tyres on their new cars

A general view

Assembling engines to chassis

had burst. Some cars did not even get ten miles from the Works before disaster. The contract was cancelled and supplies hurriedly obtained from Dunlop.

"In 1922 a change was made in the type of engine fitted. John Dorman, the designer of the Dorman 4KNO hitherto used, had designed a new engine to supersede the 4KNO. However, he had been in dispute with his fellow directors at Dormans and he finally broke with them and joined Henry Meadows Ltd. of Wolverhampton. He already knew the Company well as the 4KNO was often supplied with gearbox of Meadows' manufacture (not to Hamptons who made their own

Chassis Assembly

The Machine Shop

One of twelve Hampton chassis forming the framework of storage shed.

Hampton Works Outing to Torquay

gearboxes). John Dorman was accompanied in his move by Mr. Crump, Chief Draughtsman at Dormans, and they took with them the new engine design. This was announced by Meadows in March 1922 and described in the motoring press as the Meadows-Dorman engine. Dorman and Crump remained with Meadows for many years and were responsible for the classic 12/40 engine which powered many fine cars from 1925 up to the late 1930's. This Meadows-Dorman engine must have proved unsuccessful in some way because in September a re-designed engine was announced without the Dorman appellation. Possiblythe Dorman Company had objected to it. "This Meadows engine, in 9.8 hp. sizes was to power Hamptons until about 1930, though the 12/40 version was used when it became available in 1925. Mr. Daniel always preferred the old type 4KNO Dorman engine to the Meadows, considering it to be livelier and a better "puller" at low speeds. In 1923 Hampton's financial position was

Cyril and Dorothy Minett

The View Room Staff

Cyril Minett joined Hampton's in 1922 aged 15 years to learn the trade of viewing and inspection. He remembers his principal job as a "burrer" - removing burrs from gears and other components. He was paid 7/6 ($37\frac{1}{2}$ p) for a 48 hour week including Saturday mornings. He cycled to work from the same cottage in which he now lives in Leonard Stanley. Sadly, his wife, Dorothy, passed away whilst this book was in preparation. Cyril left in April 1924 to pursue a successful career on the railways - much later becoming the signalman at Dudbridge station. Despite his early exposure to cars he never obtained a driving licence nor owned a motor vehicle.

Hamptons nearing completion. Thomas Joseph on left.

poor. The Company was running at a loss and more capital was needed. Sir John was in a position to provide this but he felt that other Directors were not doing their share and he was unwilling to invest further sums without financial support from them. Finally, it was decided to go into voluntary liquidation and a Receiver was appointed. It was not Sir John's intention to relinquish control. He planned to come to an arrangement with the firm's creditors, buy the Company free of liabilities and form a new Company.

"The Receiver was obliged to invite bids from outsiders and many prospective purchasers came and inspected the Works. The time limited for bids expired one day at noon and that morning a Directors meeting was held. As far as Sir John knew no firm bid had been made. Mr. Myrddin Daniel urged his father to put in a bid but he refused, presumably in the hope that he would be able to buy at a lower price after the expiry date. Mr. Daniel was very anxious as he was convinced that one of the Directors had put in a personal bid without informing his fellow Directors. The meeting became very angry. Sir John refused to believe his son's story or that a colleague would go behind his back. Eventually, Sir John lost his temper and asked him to leave the meeting which he did.

"Events proved Myrddin to be right and the Daniel family lost control of the Company."

Reference to the series of photographs taken late in 1922 provides an excellent idea of the manufacturing capability of the Company but careful examination of these pictures reveals some of the "departments" overlapped and were in fact the same areas with the products and activities re-orientated presumably to impress the ultimate viewer.

The Hampton chassis with their 3/4 elliptic rear suspension anchor points are clearly visible in the photographs and were superseded a couple of years later by the semi-elliptic design.

Consequently, a dozen of the obsolete type were sent for scrap in the mid Twenties and recently came to light as the framework of a storage shed still in regular use in the Dudbridge area (Page 60). Only the rear eight feet can be examined as the front sections are concreted in the ground. Exhumation of one of these interesting unused chassis is a possibility in the future but the resulting information would be of only academic interest as none of our survivors used this design. So why did Hampton commission a London photographer to take such an extensive range of pictures ? As far as we know they did not appear in any brochures although one did appear in a local press feature, Industries of Gloucestershire (1923), so I suggest they were designed to attract more investors, as rumours of lack of capital were beginning to cause

The Body Shop

continued on Page 66

The centre spread from the 1922 brochure

Hampton
SALOON
LIMOUSINE
11·9 H.P.
SPECIFICATION :
Domed Roof.
1 Large Door either side.
Rear Squab Seat.
Adjustable Front Seats.
Near Front Seat to fold
"V" Wind Screen
Frameless Windows.
Automatic Window
Trimmed in
Head Cloth
Laces to
Electric
Spare Wheel, Tyres, Tools,
PRICE £650
COACH WORK
BY
W. MILLS & SONS
CHELTENHAM

W. Mills & Sons of Cheltenham produced this attractive two door saloon body for Hampton but only a small number were made owing to the high price.

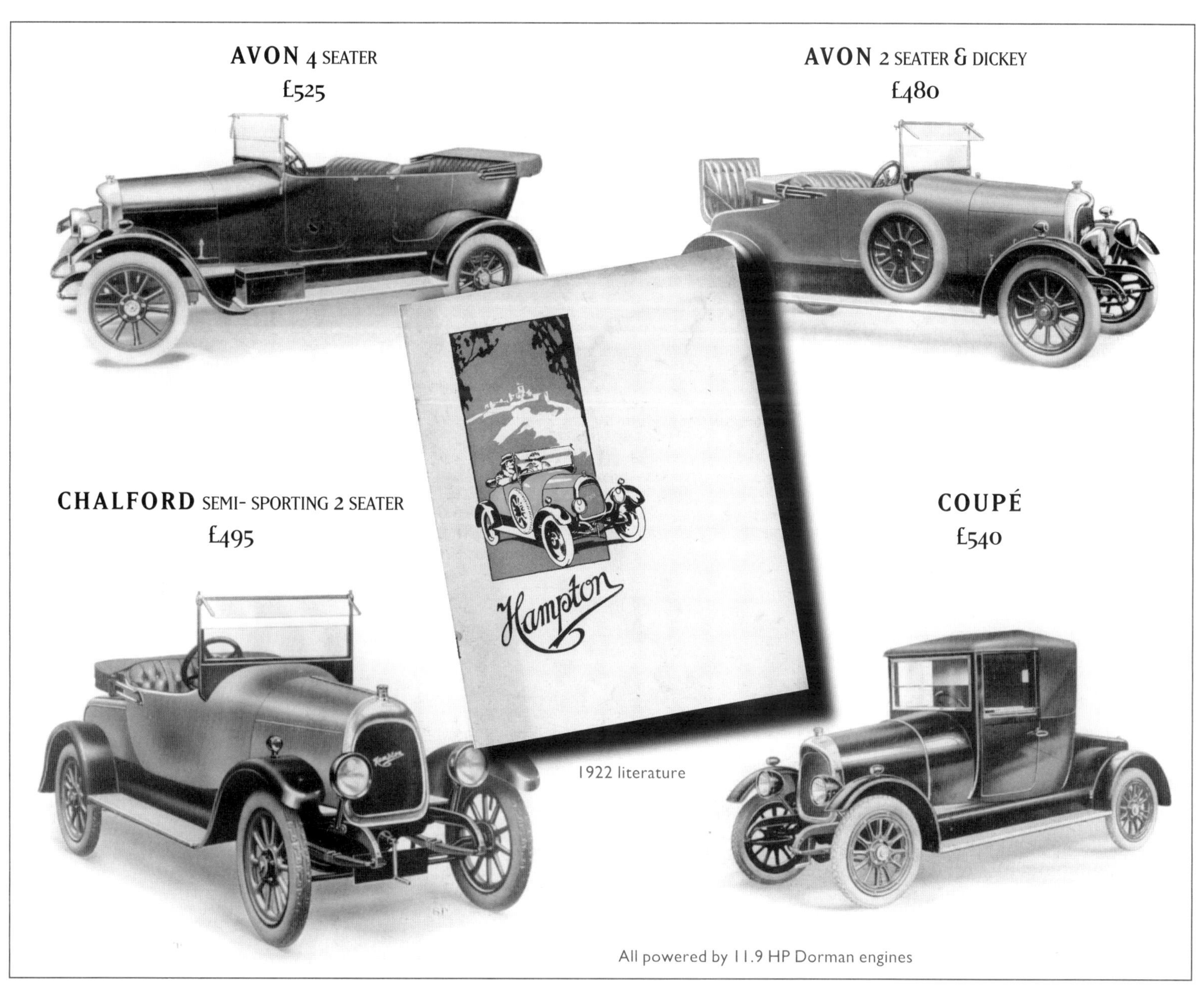

1922 literature

All powered by 11.9 HP Dorman engines

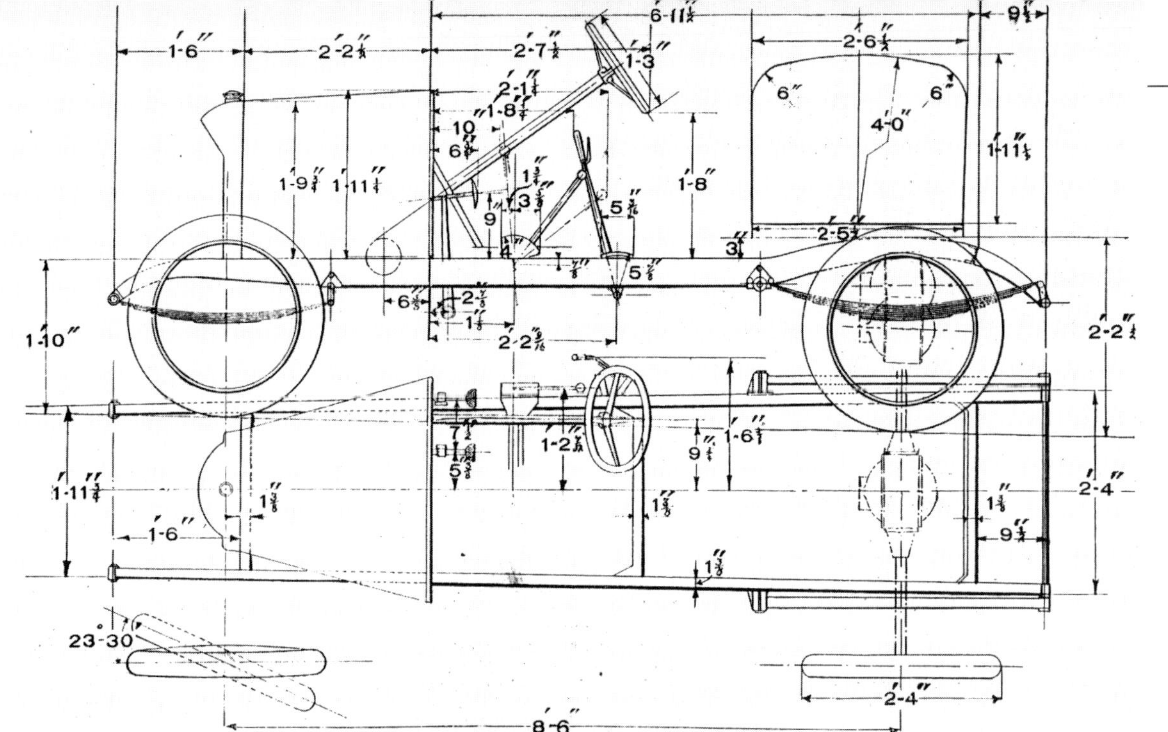

Customers wishing to have a special body made for their Hampton would be issued with a drawing similar to the 10hp chassis illustrated. Note that during 1923 the rear suspension was altered to a conventional semi elliptic layout.

serious concern once again. In July 1923 a motor salesman from Leonard Stanley, Gerald Dixon, put a further £5,000 into the Company, secured by a debenture, and some time later was given a seat on the Board.

Meanwhile, David Jones's Neath Automobile Co. was continuing to sell more cars than any other distributor (3 to 4 cars per month). One wonders if his directorship at Hamptons ensured preferential supply to his dealership. He made another interesting contribution to the Hampton cause. He was also an agent for Dennis Bros. of Guildford and was therefore in a position to loan an open charabanc to the Company for a Works Outing to Torquay in July 1923, complete with Hampton Cars livery (see Page 61), proving there were social and leisure activities taking place. One wonders on what basis the employees were selected, or perhaps it was only those who could afford a contribution. We can be sure that it was not a reward for long service.

In September 1923 Thomas Joseph left the Company after an unspecified disagreement and was replaced by William F. Milward. He was previously the Chief Engineer of W.S. Laycock Ltd., manufacturer of the Charron-Laycock car which he had helped to design. Shortly afterwards his friend, R.W. Pradier, joined him from Laycocks to become Works Manager. They had both competed in the Charron-Laycock Works team in the 200 mile race at Brooklands in 1921. They badly needed a good salesman to complete their management team and were successful in recruiting John Leno from Stewart and Ardern.

However, what the Company really needed more than anything was further capital and financial stability to fund their expansion.

As indicated by Myrrdin Daniel, a Receiver and Manager was eventually appointed on 18th March 1924. It is questionable whether this was in fact done on a voluntary basis but nevertheless John Herbert Baker from Gloucester was

R.W Pradier. At the wheel of a race prepared Charron-Laycock in 1921.

now in charge and effectively running the Company. This gentleman prepared detailed reports for Companies House and they are in fact the only internal trading information that has survived throughout the total history of Hampton Cars. They cover the period from 19th March to 6th May 1924 and therefore we are able to get a brief snapshot of the trading situation. Some of the more important facts are as follows :

25 vehicles were sold at an average price of £255 each. The dealers concerned were C.D. Ingleby of Leeds (4) Elmwood Garage (3) A.H. Meldrum of Denbigh (2) G. Madill & Co. of Belfast (2) Willcocks & Sons (2) plus 12 others from all parts of the country who purchased one each. Hampton had almost 50 agents at this time.

The principal suppliers were Henry Meadows (engine and gearbox); Dunlop & Michelin (tyres); Rudge (wheels) and Brolt or Lucas (electrics). The Company was paying rent to Apperly, Curtis at the rate of £750 per annum.

William Milward's salary was £500 per annum and John Leno claimed £7 per week travelling expenses. The Midland Bank were now the Company bankers and interestingly the Receiver did manage to pay back £10,000 to the Welsh debenture holders. Looking at such a short (49 day) period cannot reveal a complete picture but we know that the Receiver, John Baker, was paid £550 remuneration, plus £52-10-0 for carrying on business for the purchasers, plus expenses.

However by 23rd May 1924 he had sold the business on a "going concern" basis to a new company called The Stroud Motor Manufacturing Co. Ltd., bringing to an end the 3 years 4 months of Welsh ownership during which they supplied some 514 vehicles. The directors were Gerald Dixon and Major John Griffiths Jones, the gentleman who revealed himself to be the "Judas" referred to earlier - perhaps Daniel did not consider it wise to name him some 30 years ago. Dixon himself was designated sales director and Milward, general manager, probably also fulfilling the executive role of managing director. John Leno was given the job of Outside Sales. Pradier had moved on by this time.

The dismal problems suffered by Hampton Cars during the first half of 1924 must have been somewhat disturbing to the people trying to produce cars and market them. However, the new regime was creating new brochures, putting out press releases and trying very hard to re-establish their credibility. Milward and Leno were in reality a new team so they set about the task of delivering a reliable service with considerable vigour.

It is important to recognise that the Receiver (Baker) was still visiting the factory and dealing with the affairs of Hampton Engineering Co. (1920) Ltd. until 15th March 1925. Perhaps surprisingly, he also acted as Receiver for Gerald Dixon who held a secondary debenture.

5
Motor Sport and the Hampton - Sales promotion or just having fun.

The 1921 Baughan Cyclecar MD264

In the early years of motoring the participants in the new craze of motor sport were mostly from the hunting, shooting and fishing brigade - or the sons of same - as motoring was relatively expensive. After the novelty of getting successfully from A to B had worn off, motorists with a competitive outlook were seeking to display their skills in motoring competitions. One type of event to evolve was the sporting trial at which drivers of the day could pit their wits and their cars against muddy hills and unmade roads.

NAILSWORTH LADDER

From the Nailsworth valley a road climbs steeply to Minchinhampton Common via a twisting series of hairpin bends called the Nailsworth "W". Near the bottom of the hill, a rough, narrow and very steep track, 220 yards long, goes directly up the side of the hill to rejoin the road near the top. No normal motorist would dream of attempting to take his car up this forbidding climb for not only has the middle section a gradient of one in two and a half but the surface is stony,

1914 - Hampton's first climb, driven by William Paddon.

slimy in wet weather and, worst of all, has several steps of rock which threaten to break the springs of the stoutest vehicle. Nevertheless, since motoring began, there have been drivers who have enjoyed pitting their driving skill and the qualities of their cars against such hazards.

William Paddon, however, decided to bring his new 1914 creation, the Hampton Car, down to Gloucestershire for more positive reasons than pure enjoyment: climbing Nailsworth Ladder was his objective. This particular test had become a favourite venue in sporting trials of the day for both cars and motor cycles and as can be seen from the diagram was a severe climb. Local people turned out in great numbers to watch and enjoy the antics of a wide variety of competitors attempting to make clean ascents of the Ladder.

Paddon's 10hp Hampton with spartan wings and bodywork and powered by a Chapuis-Dornier engine was successful along with a Singer, Warren-Lambert and a Morgan. This success encouraged Paddon to re-visit the hill a few days later for more publicity shots to promote his new marque. He enlisted the help of the founder of Wicliffe Motor Co., Frederick Smith, with the photographs, one of which can be seen on Page 73. The original of this still hangs proudly on Wicliffe's office wall. Hence was born the idea for various slogans : "Hampton the Hill Climber", "Master of the Hills" and more. In later advertising the hill climbing attribute was applied more to its home in the Cotswold hills in general as distinct from competitive events.

After the war the Light Car and Cyclecar Magazine vigorously promoted the

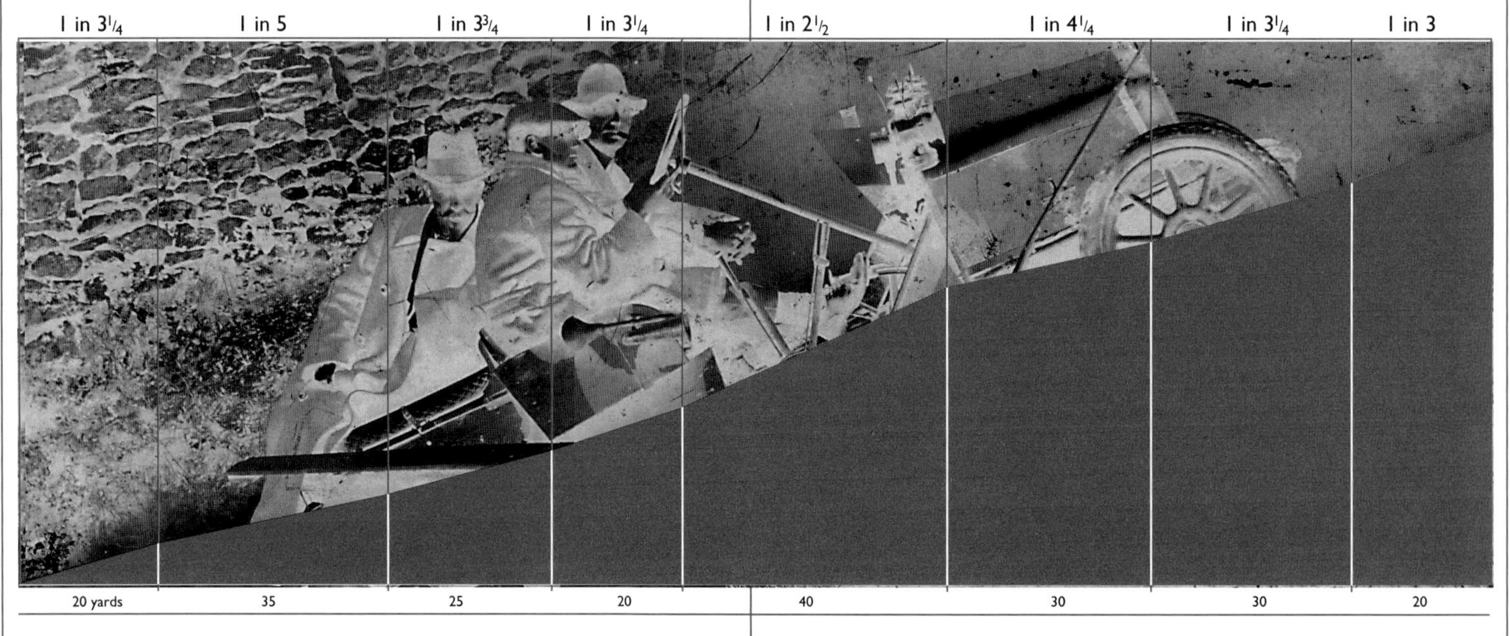

The gradient of Nailsworth Ladder.

Annual Nailsworth Ladder August event with both previews and reports accompanied by two page spreads of action photographs. Having spent the previous night assembling the chassis, Paddon was again competing with two passengers in 1919. The car now had the new Dorman ohv engine and was sporting the more familiar post-war radiator cowl. In 1920, Paddon himself did not compete, probably due to the storm clouds gathering at Dudbridge, but Starr's 10hp Hampton kept up Hampton's tradition of clean ascents and to demonstrate total supremacy carried six passengers up the hill, one more than anyone else. History was made when Mrs. Lionel Martin became the first lady driver to climb the Ladder in her husband's Aston Martin.

1921 saw many more successful climbs including Sir John Daniel's son Myrddin who climbed the hill several times, finally carrying fourteen brave souls including himself. A static photograph was taken for publicity purposes (see Page 75) but by now this strange behaviour was beginning to appear ridiculous - more of a circus act than enjoyable motor sport. To further illustrate the point eighteen people then scrambled into a 20hp Dodge car to make a clean ascent. At least three Hampton employees, Messrs. Scolefield, Dawkins and Albert Moore, (the patternmaker) worked hard as "scotchers" on the hill that day. The motoring press claimed that 4,000 people enjoyed the weekend's entertainment.

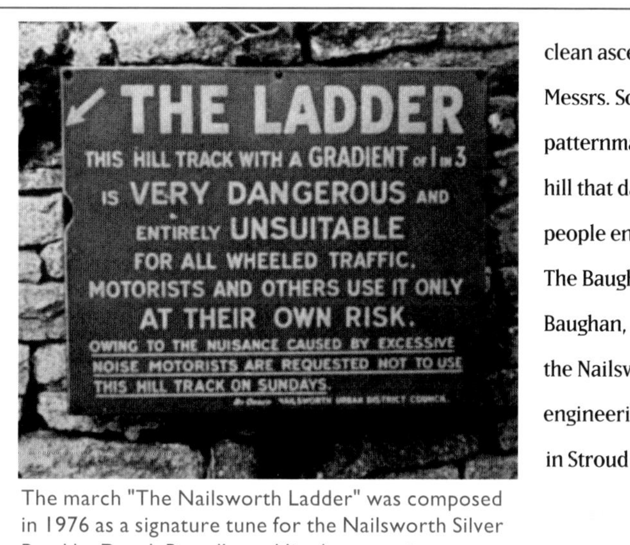

The march "The Nailsworth Ladder" was composed in 1976 as a signature tune for the Nailsworth Silver Band by Derek Broadbent. His chart topping arrangement of "The Floral Dance" featuring the Brighouse & Rastrick Band became a household favourite with a little assistance from disc jockey, Terry Wogan.

The Baughan Cyclecar, driven by its creator Harry Baughan, was a successful, regular competitor on the Nailsworth Ladder. His engineering company in Stroud occasionally carried out subcontract machining for Hamptons. Cyclecars and motor cycles were only a fringe activity of Baughan (Stroud) Ltd. who are still in business, manufacturing plastic and rubber extrusion machinery. The detailed history of Harry Baughan is being compiled by Stroud enthusiast, Ken Chandler, who plans to cover all aspects of this pioneering engineer's life. Harry Baughan built the first of his six cyclecars in Middlesex in 1920 using the registration number **MD 264**. He came to the West Country in 1922 and set up his engineering business in Lower Street, Stroud. His surviving car has been used in many VSCC competitions including trials, sprints, hill climbs and driving tests in the hands of its present owner, Pat Mather, since it first climbed the Nailsworth Ladder in 1921, then with a tandem passenger seat. The original car was designed along aircraft lines (reflecting Baughan's early employment at De Havillands) using a series of wire tensioners covered with a fabric body treated with "dope". When this finally disintegrated it was re-skinned with light alloy and re-designed to accommodate a passenger next to the driver.

Harry Baughan at the wheel of MD 264 - 1921

Present brief specification of Baughan cyclecar

Engine:	JAP - 90 degree V - twin. 1000cc side valve, Amal carburettor. Magneto ignition.
Clutch:	Twin plate - dry cork
Transmission:	Morris Oxford 3 speed and reverse gearbox driving a Bevel box with chain drive to a solid rear axle.
Chassis:	5.1/2" x 3/4" ash frame. Quarter elliptic springs front and rear. No spring dampers.

Without doubt the 1921 Junior Car Club meeting at the Ladder provided a good social weekend and was enjoyed by everyone. It included a dinner and impromptu concert at the Imperial Hotel, Stroud on the Saturday evening.

Young Daniel's Welsh vocal chords were well exercised with at least two popular songs that evening perhaps lubricated with some fine ale from Godsell's brewery. When the fun was all over, Hampton's future surely lay in improving their productivity and finding ways to climb many of the formidable financial and

JAP engine 90° V-twin

Frederick Smith, with cigarette, the founder of Wicliffe Motor Co. Ltd. with William Paddon on The Ladder. 1914

economic mountains that faced all motor manufacturers at that time. However, Nailsworth Ladder has endured and it is still used today for trials including the famous Cotswold Clouds event.

10-16 H·P Two-Seater
Complete —— £520
Hampton
The FIRST and ONLY Car with 2, 3 and 4 passengers to climb the NAILSWORTH LADDER,
—a gradient of 1 in 2·5.
Can easily do 50 miles per hour.
SPECIFICATION ABRIDGED.
CHASSIS.—Frame of Pressed Steel. Springs, front ½ elliptic, rear ¾ elliptic. Wheelbase 9 ft.
ENGINE.—10-16 h.p. (1496 c.c.'s), bore 63 mm., stroke 120 mm., overhead valves, of large area, embodying latest aero engine practice, adjustable tappets.
COOLING.—Thermo-Syphon.
LUBRICATION.—Forced fed lubrication.
CARBURETTER.—Zenith-Claudel automatic vertical type.
MAGNETO.—All-British Watford Magneto, high tension watertight, enclosed type.
CLUTCH.—Leather to metal.
GEARBOX.—Three speeds and reverse.
TRANSMISSION.—Bevel drive, special type.
BRAKES.—Foot and side brakes, both actuating on the rear wheels. Thus no brake strain comes on transmission.
WHEELS AND TYRES.—710 x 90, Sankey Steel, detachable and interchangeable spare wheel included in the set. Dunlop Magnum Tyres, with spare tyre.
BODY.—Low built, upholstered leather, folding hood, single dicky seat.
LIGHTING AND STARTING.—Lucas or Broit Dynamo Electric Equipment.
Send for Catalogue giving full Specification.
'Phone— 108 Stroud
'Grams— "Widawak, Stroud."
1 in 2·5

Clean Ladder ascents by year.

1914

10 hp Singer
8 hp Warren-Lambert
8 hp Morgan
10 hp Hampton

1919

8 hp Morgan
10 hp Hampton
10 hp Eric - Campbell
8 hp Carden

1920

10 hp Hampton
10 hp Warren-Lambert
10 hp Morgan
8 hp G.N.
10 hp Aston Martin
10 hp Douglas
8 hp Carden
8 hp A.V.

1921

10 hp Hampton
8.7hp Crouch
8 hp Baughan
10 hp Warren-Lambert
10 hp Enfield-Alldays Sport
8 hp T.B.
8 hp G.N.
12 hp A.B.C.
8 hp Morgan
7 hp Carden
10 hp Horstman (Sports)

William Paddon in 1919 without bonnet but with new radiator design.

Myrddin Daniel posing on the ladder with his thirteen workers. 1921

1997 - A Dellow climbs the Ladder

BROOKLANDS

Whilst taking part in sporting trials could be enjoyed in a substantially standard vehicle, motor racing was different. In the 1920's motor racing meant one word - Brooklands.

The Hampton company was not able to support a racing programme because of their delicately balanced financial position; however, one of their major distributors, B.S. Marshall of London, obviously thought the publicity and contacts that derive from racing would be worth pursuing. Bertie Marshall first entered a 1795cc Dorman engined Hampton in the Essex Motor Club's August meeting in 1921. The race was a 5¾ mile Senior Short Handicap in which he was not placed. However, he went on to record some good results in 1922 as summarised in our panel. He was quick to place an advertisement in The Autocar in April 1922 (Page 81) proclaiming that "The Aesthetic Hampton has Power as well as Grace" and then in the smaller print "driving a practically

Bertie Marshall driving the 1795 cc special bodied Hampton Racing Car

Hampton - No. 8

standard 11.9hp Hampton".

An examination of the special chassis with artillery wheels (later replaced with wire wheels) and light weight body will indicate significant deviation from the standard product. His racing engine Dorman No. 12543 with the twin Zenith carburettors feeding a twin inlet port cylinder head plus lightened flywheel may help explain why he was performing much better in 1922 than the previous season.

However, as most of the races were handicaps it would not be too long before the officials adjusted his figures to suit his improved performance. After all, everybody else would have been making similar tuning adjustments. Later in the season he achieved 82.86 mph which must qualify him for driving the fastest 4 cylinder Hampton on record. In subsequent years he drove a variety of other cars including Crouch and Brescia Bugattis with considerable success.

H.G. Munton was racing mechanic to B.S. Marshall in the Twenties and in conversation with Bill Boddy, MBE in 1963, he recounted many of his experiences including the following paragraph which appeared in Motor Sport.

"Marshall also drove the special racing Hampton, prepared by the makers, but the 2-bearing crankshaft of its Dorman type KNO engine was the limiting factor, at more than 89 m.p.h. on Brooklands. In fact, on one occasion Munton was driving away from the track with an engineer from Dorman's, who had come down to see whether the engine could be improved, beside him when at Thames Ditton a queer noise intruded. Opening the bonnet Munton noticed a bent rocker so he removed it, cut out the plug to that cylinder and drove on to London on three. In fact, when the engine was stripped, he found that the crankshaft had broken and was in two pieces, still by a fluke revolving as one !"

The Racing Hampton chassis - pictured outside the office block at the Dudbridge Works.

Chassis of the Brooklands Car

Frame	Lower than standard with upsweep over the rear axle.
Springs	Half elliptic at rear instead of three quarter elliptic on the production model.
Engine	Set further back in frame. Twin carburettors & inlet ports..
Clutch Pedal) Brake Pedal)	Drilled to save weight
Gear change lever) Hand brake lever)	Repositioned to give more rearward driving seat
Steering column	Lengthened and raked
Front axle	Entirely different design, lacking the dip in the centre which features on the standard axle.
Radiator	Considerably larger than standard.
Springs	Bound with whipcord to increase friction between the leaves - a common device on competition cars before the introduction of shock absorbers.
Brakes	Drums enlarged and finned to improve cooling.

Interestingly, Lionel Martin whom he beat in 1922 in his Aston Martin at the Easter Monday Race was having fun just 8 months earlier on the Nailsworth Ladder. Marshall's exploits at Brooklands would also have brought him into contact with Leno, Pradier and Milward before they became involved with Hampton Cars.

It is refreshing to observe that Marshall and his Hampton were mixing with many of the legends of the Brooklands motor racing fraternity including Malcolm Campbell, Count Zborowski, Kaye Don, Wolf Barnato, Henry Seagrave and Parry Thomas to name just a few.

Whilst Marshall's racing Hampton was a private venture some financial and engineering support was provided by the Dudbridge Works. This would have been mainly as a goodwill gesture to their principal London dealer who was

Rear suspension, showing revised layout

well known to Sir John Daniel. Racing at Brooklands was part of the apprenticeship for young men who wished to pursue a career in the fast evolving motor industry. John Leno in his Bébé Peugeot raced in 1913/14 and Pradier and Milward were both seen as Works drivers competing in October 1921 in smart 1.5 litre Charron-Laycock models. (The 200 mile race).

Successful race results for 1922. From 5 Meetings - 19 Races

17th April	3rd in 75mph	Short handicap	5.3/4 miles
	1st in 75mph	Long handicap	8.1/2 miles
13th May	3rd in 75mph	Short handicap	5.3/4 miles
	2nd in 75mph	Long handicap	8.1/2 miles
5th June	2nd in 90mph	Long handicap	8.1/2 miles
	2nd in 75mph	Long handicap	8.1/2 miles

The lightened and lowered front suspension.

NINTH RACE.

DISTANCE : ABOUT 8½ MILES. (Pond Start. Special Short Finishing Line.)

(Cars will pass the fork twice, and then enter the straight.)

4.50 p.m. THE SEVENTEENTH 75 M.P.H. LONG HANDICAP. (The entrant of the winn[er] Cup, value £30, the entrant of the second a Cup, value £15; and the entrant of the thir[d] £10. Two to start or no race; five to start, or no second prize; seven to start, or no third prize.) For motor cars in racing trim, propelled by means of internal combustion engines only, exceeding 1,1[...]

Entrance 5 sov. Closed 3rd April, 1922.

No.	Entrant.	Vehicle.	Bore.	Stroke	Cubic Capacity.	Driver.	Colour of Ca[r]
1	Capt. C. A. Glentworth	Essex	85·7	127	2,930	J. S. Cauldrey	Grey, Black wheels
2	Mr. H. R. S. Birkin	D.F.P.	70	130	2,001	W. D. Hawkes	Light Blue
3	Mr. Lionel Martin	Aston-Martin II.	66·5	107	1,487	Lionel Martin	Black
4	Mr. Woolf Barnato	Ansaldo	72	120	1,954	Woolf Barnato	Red
3 5	Mr. A. J. McCormack	Wolseley	65	95	1,261	Capt. A. G. Miller	Aluminium
1 6	Mr. B. S. Marshall	Hampton	69	120	1,795	B. S. Marshall	Black
2 7	Mr. T. B. Andre	Marlborough	60·5	120	1,380	T. B. Andre	Red, Black wheel[s]
8	Mr. J. W. Tollady	Crouch (2-cyl.)	86	95	1,115	J. W. Tollady	Primrose, Blue w[heels]
9	Mr. E. C. G. England	A.B.C. (2-cyl.)	91·5	91·5	1,203	E. C. G. England	Red, Black whe[els]

Prize winners of any previous handicap at this Meeting may be re-handicapped at the discretion of t[he]

RESULT.

Winner 6 *Second* 7 *Third* 5

Bertie Marshall - the winner.

BROOKLANDS AUTOMOBILE RACING CLUB.

OFFICIAL RACE CARD.

PRICE ONE SHILLING.

EASTER MONDAY, APRIL 17TH, 1922.

This Race Card is published for the Executive by HARRISON & SONS, LTD., of St. Martin's Lane, and is only to be obtained of the Official Card Sellers on the Course.

continued on Page 81

The Hampton Factory and Office Block in Selsley Hill (1927-31). Demolished Autumn 1996.

Hampton Motor Cycle - 1912

Specification

Engine : T.D. Cross 500 CC single cylinder side valve

Brown Barlow Carburettor

Bosch Magneto   Sturmey Archer Hub Clutch

Phillipson two speed engine pulley

Brampton Forks - Brooks saddle

Lucas carbide lighting.

The Hampton Motor Cycle has been used on several London - Brighton runs in recent years and is owned by Mr. Jack Light.

Mr. & Mrs. Milward on the Brecon Beacons.

The Milward Hampton returns to Blenheim House 65 years after it was built there. 8th March 1997.

Stroud Show. 1966.

HW 2734 at Dudbridge for the opening of Sainsbury's. 5th March 1997

72 THE AUTOCAR. ADVERTISEMENTS. APRIL 29TH, 1922.

Easter *Hampton* Successes

MR. B. S. MARSHALL, driving a practically STANDARD 11.9 H.P. HAMPTON at Brooklands on Easter Monday secured:

1st Place in the 75 M.P.H. Long Handicap
3rd Place „ „ 75 M.P.H. Short Handicap

The Aesthetic Hampton

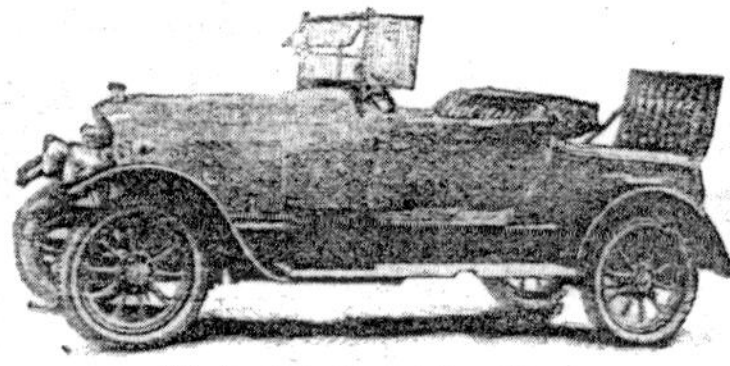

has Power as well as Grace.

Sole Agents London and Home Counties:

B. S. MARSHALL, Ltd., 17A, Hanover Square, W.1

'Phone: MAYFAIR 5906.

ALSO AGENTS FOR MATHIS, WOLSELEY, SINGER, A-C, F.N., CHANDLER, AND ROAMER.

GENERAL COMPETITIONS

Whilst Hamptons were never in a position to offer sports models or tuned cars to their normal customers, the lively general performance of the standard cars with their willing ohv engines, 4 speed gearboxes and generally solid engineering made them popular for use in weekend motor sport and other reliability events. Press reports frequently mentioned Hamptons taking part and performing well in a variety of Motor Club promotions throughout the British Isles.

Situated in North Yorkshire, the Sutton Bank Hill Climb in August 1920 featured two Hamptons. Macilvane's car making a steady climb in 2 mins. 34.4 secs. in contrast to Felix Scriven's swashbuckling style which totally dominated his class with a very fast time of 2 mins. 13.5 secs. Felix was a regular Hampton competitor in the North of England before making a name for himself in his well known Brooklands Austin 20 racer, known as "Sergeant Murphy".

John Leno (with goggles) 1913. Essex Motor Club Brooklands Meeting.

Milward (46) and Pradier (29) prior to their Brooklands debut.

FP 893 Felix Scriven's early Hampton with special doorless body, circa 1919

John Leno entered the testing Scottish Thousand Miles Trial and, at the other end of the country, the M.C.C. London to Lands End Trial in his hard working Hampton **DD3218** picking up Gold medals in both.

In the early Twenties, largely due to the vigorous sales efforts of David T. Jones at the Neath & District Automobile Co., South Wales boasted more Hamptons than other areas, so it was not surprising that a dozen Hamptons turned out for the Porthcawl Sands Speed Trial at Rest Bay on August 6th 1921. The organisers, The Cardiff Motor Cycle Club, had extended the event to include motor cars - probably encouraged by Sir John Daniel who had donated several silver cups for the competition.

The large entry of Hamptons would no doubt have been linked to Sir John's gesture which would have been publicised through his dealerships.

As far as we know this event was the nearest Hampton Cars ever came to establishing an Owners Club. Our photograph from "The Autocar" (overleaf) is unique but sadly the original negative has not survived so we are not able to identify the cars or their drivers, although at least two seem to have the larger type of trade plates - Works cars perhaps ? The results were published in The Porthcawl News which revealed that Sir John himself competed and that his son, Myrddin, collected an award for fastest Hampton in the 1500cc class (second place). Bertie Marshall's Hampton, almost predictably, won the 1825cc class and also recorded the fastest time of the day. No doubt a good day out for our Hamptons and a satisfactory sales promotion exercise for Sir John.

The only other competition car regularly to remind enthusiasts of Hampton's existence is the 1925 Cognac Special, developed and raced with considerable success by the late Ron Footitt. Its familiar radiator, the only Hampton component, is known to all followers of vintage motor sport.

Possibly the very last Hampton to compete was **YC 6058** when it appeared at the Silverstone Circuit in 1956 - perhaps in a half hour trial or short handicap race - sadly this car has not been seen for many years, presumed scrapped. Its last known owners were Ron Radford and a Mr. Hobbs of Ancaster in 1959.

HAMPTON JUNIOR

9-21 h.p.

First Appearance in Competition.

LONDON——EDINBURGH.

1 Car Entered. 1 Gold Medal.

The above Car was driven by Capt. Hunter, of Exeter.

KIRKSTONE PASS. Hunter (Hampton) was excellent.

Vide page 678 *The Motor*, May 22nd.

Climbing Beggar's Roost. John Leno in the MCC Lands End Trial 1924.

Sir John Daniel's Hampton, driven by Myrddin Daniel, competing at Catsash Hill Climb, near Newport. He finished third in the 1500cc class behind a Hillman and a G.N.

Rest Bay, Porthcawl. August 1921. A dozen Hamptons.

Hampton Cars

The Ideal Ladies' Car is the Car that is First of All.

RELIABLE.

PROOF.—Captain F. J. C. Hunter, of Exeter, who purchased a Hampton Car 3 years ago, was awarded a Gold Medal in this year's London—Land's End Run, repeating his success of last year, when he won a Silver Medal in the London—Land's End Run and a Gold Medal in the London—Edinburgh Run. This car has already done 32,000 miles, thus proving reliability

This is one of the few Hampton advertisements aimed at the lady driver. No doubt Rosa Ward and later Bonnie Monro would have testified to the cars' suitability for their use.

Unfortunately, our Porthcawl picture is not clear enough to identify any ladies preparing to demonstrate their skill at Rest Bay.

The Cognac Special driven by Ron Footitt at The Prescott Hill Climb August 1973

No.2. NL 5321 An unknown competitor

No.45. DD 5504 Hampton. Perhaps Gerald Dixon at the wheel

YC 6058 - The last Hampton to enter a race ?

6
A change of name - A change of fortune?

John Leno seated in the Bébé Peugeot.

Dixon, Milward and Leno worked hard during the remainder of 1924 to re-build the business, advertising extensively "The Return of the Hampton", and encouraging the cars' use in trials and other motor sport. Major J.G. Jones, the other director, did not appear to occupy any executive role in the company, presumably still residing in Wales.

Excellent News!

The return of the Hampton

WE have acquired the whole of the assets of the Hampton Engineering Co. with a view to regaining for the car that popularity which is so justly its due.

From the particulars and prices shown below, the discriminating buyer will appreciate that — always a car of sterling quality — Hampton value is now unsurpassed.

We guarantee the refund to any purchaser of any price reduction which may take place between the present date and October 15 next.

John Leno was a colourful character perhaps inheriting his sense of humour from his famous father, Dan Leno, the Edwardian comedian. On leaving school he was apprenticed to the Premier Motor Cycle Co. in Aston, Birmingham and was actively involved with their early two stroke motor cycles. Later he moved to the London area and just before the war became sales manager of Peugeot (England) Ltd., frequently being seen in the pretty Bébé Peugeot designed by Ettore Bugatti. He raced a highly tuned Bébé at Brooklands in 1913 in the first ever race for cyclecars, and followed this with a 3rd place in 1914.

Leno astride the 3.5 Premo motor cycle - 1908

The Stroud Motor Manufacturing Co. Ltd. chose the London Motor Show at Olympia to introduce their two new 14hp models alongside three 10hp models. These featured the Henry Meadows 2120cc ohv engine with 75mm bore x 120mm stroke together with the Meadows 5A four speed gearbox. Four wheel braking was available on all models as on the show cars but rear wheel braking only was still an option at lower cost. The double brake shoes at the rear were retained along with the three quarter elliptic rear springing.

The two seater chassis had a 9 foot 1 inch wheelbase while the four seater was one foot longer. Interestingly, the engines for these two cars only arrived on the 3rd October so one can imagine the considerable effort that must have been made to present them in show condition in just two to three weeks.

Their handsome, illustrated brochure, printed by Frederick Steel & Co. of Ebley especially for the Show, gives the full specifications of all these models. The cover design with colour picture of Rodborough Fort as a background is

John Leno pushes the 1925 model 10hp Hampton coupé through the doors of Olympia for the 1924 Motor Show. No help from the British working man !

particularly pleasing - as is the die-stamped red logo Hampton Cars.

Strangely, they halted production of the popular 12hp cars whilst engineering the new 14hp models. Regrettably, their brave effort to move up the market place failed badly and only eleven 14hp cars were sold in 1924/5. However, the sales success of the smaller 10hp cars, called the Junior or the T.10, was quite impressive during 1924 when some 136 cars were sold. Meanwhile, in the factory, the workforce, although a little bewildered by another management change, were continuing to build and test cars. Albert Waite was the chief test driver and had been with the company from the early days. He was considered to be very knowledgeable and his son, Fred, became his assistant. Albert was also an ingenious engineering inventor and prior to his Hampton days, designed and built a special motor cycle sidecar to carry eggs collected from local farms. See Page 94.

Nevertheless, in 1925 the Press, seemingly out of touch with reality, were saying complimentary things about the Company, particularly William Milward who obviously impressed a reporter from The Auto (12th March 1925) who said :

"The Hampton and Mr. W.F. Milward.

"I was pleased to see, in the issue of February 26 last, that the member of our staff who deals with road trials had made acquaintance with the new Hampton, which should by rights be called the Milward Hampton. Mr. Duffield said, toward the conclusion of his notes upon a test of this excellent little job, "I do not know what Mr. Milward is called, in his relationship to the company producing the Hampton; but I know what his designation should be."

"For the benefit of my colleague, and of others similarly unaware of recent Hampton history, I may say that Mr. W.F. Milward, AMIME, MSAE, and so on, is general manager to the Stroud Motor Manufacturing Co. Ltd. and exercises all the functions of general managership, in design, production and sales. He is in other words, in absolute charge of the works at Dudbridge. Not long ago Hampton cars were faced by all sorts of bad luck, commercially speaking, though they remained good little cars. A receivership was in operation in March, 1924, but at about the end of July a new company was formed and in the past six or eight months Mr. Milward has very abundantly justified his appointment as general manager, one which the directors made about 14 months ago.

"Mr. Milward is relatively a young man, best known by the Charron-Laycock which he designed. Much of the 1925 Hampton models' design is his own work, so much so that he is content to be regarded as responsible for it; but a lot of his success springs from the fact that he is not only a good engineer, but is also a good salesman, with a clear idea of what the average car-buyer really wants."

continued on Page 94

Stroud Motor Manufacturing Co. Limited

Mechanical Specifications

	10hp	14hp
Chassis	High tensile steel frame, 3.5" section. Wheelbase 8 ft 8 ins. track 4ft.	High tensile steel frame, 4.5" section. Wheelbase 9 ft. (2-seater & coupé) 10 ft. (4 seater) track 4 ft.
Engine	Overhead valve, 4 cylinder engine, with 4 speed gearbox, unit construction. 63 bore x 100 stroke m/m, 9.8 RAC rating. Petrol consumption 40/45 mpg. Adjustable tappets.	Overhead valve, 4 cylinder engine, with 4 speed gearbox, unit construction. 75 bore x 120 stroke m/m. 13.9 RAC rating. Petrol consumption 30/35 mpg. Adjustable tappets, detachable head.
Cooling	Thermo syphon with efficient radiator, suitable for all climates.	As 10 hp.
Lubrication	Trough lubrication to every engine bearing, the supply of oil being maintained by pump in sump.	Force feed lubrication to every engine bearing by pump in sump.
Carburettor	Zenith	As 10 hp
Magneto	High tension, B.L.I.C.	As 10 hp
Clutch	Leather to metal, cone type.	As 10 hp
Gearbox	Four speeds and reverse. Ball bearings throughout. Right hand control.	As 10 hp
Universal joints	Special design, requires no lubrication	Special design.
Transmission	Spiral bevel drive with full floating back axle.	As 10 hp
Brakes	Both foot and hand of internal expanding type in dustproof drums, both acting direct on the rear wheels. When 4 wheel brakes are fitted these also of internal expanding type; they are inter-connected to pair of rear brakes, operated by foot pedal, thus making 6 brakes in all. All brake shoes are lined with die pressed Ferodo.	Foot and side internal expanding in dustproof drums, both acting on rear wheels. Right-hand control.
Springs	Front and rear specially long, half elliptic.	Front, half elliptic. Rear, three quarter elliptic. All with gaiters.
Steering	Worm and sector, irreversible.	As 10 hp
Controls	Foot accelerator. Hand controls for throttle & ignition mounted on steering column.	As 10 hp
Front axle	"H" section steel stamping	As 10 hp
Wheels	5 detachable and interchangeable steel artillery wheels for 710x90 m/m or 28x4.95 tyres.	5 detachable & interchangeable Dunlop artillery steel wheels for 760x90 m/m or 29x4.95 tyres.
Tyres	710x90 m/m Dunlop cord or 28x4.95 Balloon cord.	760x90 m/m Dunlop cord or 29x4.95 Balloon cord.
Starting & Lighting	Lucas 6 volt electric lighting and starting equipment. 5 lamps.	Lucas 12 volt electric lighting and starting equipment. 5 lamps.
Fittings	White metal and nickel plated.	All fittings white metal or nickel plated.
Equipment	Kit of tools - car jack, pump, detachable wheelbrace.	As 10 hp
Petrol tank	7 gallons, gravity fed	8 gallons. Autovac feed.

10hp		14hp
£275 4 wheel brakes extra £20. Overall Dimensions : 12' 0" long, 5' 0" wide, 5' 10" high Weight : 15.75 cwt.	***2 Seater - All Weather***	**£350** 4 wheel brakes extra £25. Overall dimensions : 12' 6" long, 5' 0" wide, 6' 1" high Weight : 19.5 cwt.
£298 4 wheel brakes extra £20 Overall Dimensions : 12' 0" long, 5' 0" wide, 6' 0" high Weight : 16.5 cwt	***4 Seater - All Weather***	**£395** 4 wheel brakes extra £25 Overall Dimensions : 13' 6" long, 5' 0" wide, 6' 6" high Weight : 20.5 cwt
£330 4 wheel brakes extra £20 Overall Dimensions : 12' 0" long, 5' 0" wide, 6' 0" high Weight : 16.5 cwt	***2 Seater Coupé and Dickey***	**£398** 4 wheel brakes extra £27 Overall Dimensions : 12' 6" long, 5' 0" wide, 6' 1" high Weight : 19.5 cwt

The Auto report was very confusing when one considers the failure of the 14hp models. Perhaps the journalist was trying to say that what the "average car buyer really wants" is smaller cars, i.e. the T.10 and the 12hp.

The management, realising their major strategic blunder, desperately tried to reverse their policy by bringing back the 12hp car early in 1925 and making it their major model. With their scaled down production capacity they could only do this by dramatically cutting back the production of the 10hp range - to a mere 21 cars in 1925.

Whilst a hundred 12hp models were sold, when October came round things at Dudbridge had become very serious. Four different 12hp models were on show at Olympia in 1925 but by the time Milward and Leno returned home from London they found a Receiver sitting on the doorstep. It seems that the Company could not live with the extremely difficult trading conditions and the severe price cutting, particularly that of William Morris with his Bullnose. His cars were around £100 cheaper than most other cars in their class. Notwithstanding this, a total of 190 Hamptons were sold during the reign of The Stroud Motor Manufacturing Co. Ltd.

P.E. Rowbotham of Cardiff was appointed Receiver by the directors and debenture holders, Major J.G. Jones and Gerald Dixon. A creditors' meeting was held in January 1926 which revealed unsecured liabilities of £23,269,

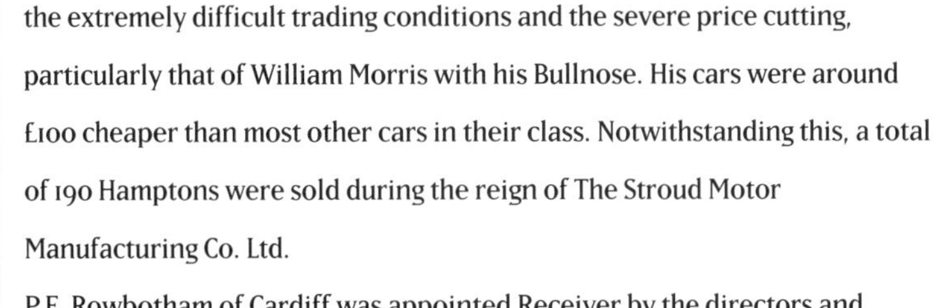

Albert & Fred Waite (1952)

BSA motor cycle fitted with Albert Waite's sidecar

including £8,500 owing to Major Jones. The assets of the company - stock, machinery etc - totalled £16,794 from which had to be deducted preferential claims of £12,470, leaving net assets of only £4,324. Major Jones offered to forego his proportion, providing all the unsecured creditors would accept 5/- (25p) in the pound - which, after discussion, they did.

Jones and Dixon were also personally guaranteeing the bank overdraft - little wonder that Jones was too ill to attend the meeting and Dixon later turned to

The semi coupé 3 seater Hampton - equally suited to golfers or long distance touring.

alcohol. It's worth noting that Henry Meadows, the engine supplier, was not on the creditors list as they had obviously withdrawn credit terms, owing to the poor payment record in the past.

The Receiver arranged for the sale of assets and winding up of the Company after a life of only 17 months. Was this the end of Hampton Cars ?

2 seater

The 12hp models on show at Olympia 1925

5 seater - de luxe

7
Badge Engineering

1928 10hp Saloon

Faced with another Receivership and seeing their new creation crash so quickly, it would be reasonable and sensible to assume that Milward and Leno would throw in the towel - as Dixon had. But it appears that once motor cars get into some people's blood, common sense ceases to exist. Milward was already talking to the elderly John Hatton-Hall, a Hampton owner, who expressed an interest in investing in a new company.

Whilst the idea of re-financing Hamptons appealed to him he was not prepared to buy the Company as a going concern but planned to follow the well established practice of the day of waiting "until the break up of the business and buying the remains at a low price."

According to Max, it was eventually an eleventh hour reprieve with Milward and Leno begging Hatton-Hall to help them and also sinking their last few personal pennies into the new Company. Thus Hampton Cars (London) Ltd. was created with its registered office now at No. 1, Central Buildings, Westminster, London SW1 with a capital of £2,500. Milward and Leno retained their directorships, presumably with Hatton-Hall becoming chairman.

The incorporation of the new entity did not take place until 30th September 1926, some six to seven months after taking over and almost a year since the last Receiver was appointed (19.10.25). A total of 38 cars were produced during 1926 - 18 sold by the Receiver of the previous regime and 20 produced by the new Company. This was the lowest annual total so far and indicative of the serious problems Hampton Cars now faced. They did not exhibit at Olympia in 1926 or 1927 although Bertie Marshall did advertise and displayed a full range of 12hp cars at his Knightsbridge premises in '27. Max had been led to believe that John Hatton-Hall was a wealthy businessman with connections in the banana producing industry of the West Indies. However, more detailed research indicates that

John Hatton-Hall. The new owner.

Dudbridge House from an early print.

1997 - Restoration has begun.

this was unlikely although both tea and rubber have been suggested as the original source of his wealth.

Together with his wife, he moved to Gloucestershire and rented a few rooms at Dudbridge House, the large family home of Wesley Whitfield. This elegant eighteenth century building was constructed for John Hawker, the wealthy mill owner and in the terms of the day "A clothier".

Hatton-Hall's purchase of the remains of The Stroud Motor Manufacturing Co. amounted to sinking his life savings into the business which perhaps explains why he came to lodge a few hundred yards from his investment.

His personal transport was a Hampton saloon model which he had decorated on each door with his coat of arms, the original design of which dates from the time of Queen Elizabeth I and had belonged to Sir Christopher Hatton (1540-1591), a close friend of the Queen and later Lord Chancellor of England.

Historians have previously made a connection between him and Sir Francis Drake, possibly because a Golden Hind is depicted at the crest of the coat of arms but substantive evidence does not appear to exist.

It is difficult to understand how John Hatton-Hall had any right to use this coat of arms as Sir Christopher did not marry and whilst Hatton-Hall may have had some vague connection with the family he is not a direct descendant; his use of the emblem was opportunistic to say the least.

However, in 1929, he incorporated it into Hampton's sales literature and also .replaced the original radiator badge with this insignia. Badge engineering of the worst kind! Strangely, it did not appear on the letterheading of the era so perhaps they had good stock of the usual type. The Latin motto *"Virtus tutissima cassis"* translates as "Virtue is the safest helmet" - perhaps ideal if you are selling motor cycles.

A new brochure was produced introducing the new Company name featuring only the 12hp model. Presumably they thought that adding London to the title would add status and credibility to the marque - characteristics which were sorely needed once again. The factory was by now far too large for the Company's requirements so the search for smaller premises was an economic necessity. This was also consistent with their desire to rationalise manufacturing away from in-house production towards greater use of proprietary parts such as rear axles and the Meadows gearbox.

In September 1927 they purchased the freehold of a large part of The Dudbridge Ironworks site (in receivership) and moved out of the specially built factory which they had been renting from Apperly, Curtis and Co. Ltd. Their erstwhile landlords were probably relieved to see them go as they only received 5/- in the pound for arrears of rent from the old company. The disruption caused by this move mostly explains why only 25 cars were sold in 1927. John Leno was busy writing to customers and mentioning the new factory to encourage further badly needed sales.

The move of about 500 yards to the other side of Dudbridge Road was

STATIONS.
G.W.R. STROUD. 1 MILE.
STONEHOUSE. 3 MILES.
L.M.S. STONEHOUSE. 3 MILES.
DUDBRIDGE. ½ MILE.

YOUR REF.
OUR REF.

All letters to be addressed to the Firm and not to individuals.

PROPRIETORS
HAMPTON CARS (LONDON) LTD.
DUDBRIDGE. - - - STROUD. GLOS.

Telephone: Nos 271 STROUD.
Telegrams: 271 STROUD.

C. Sutton Esq.   10th October 1927.
Marloes Road, W.1.

Dear Sir,

As an old HAMPTON owner we feel sure you will be interested to hear that we have recently purchased the Freehold of the Dudbridge Iron Works and are now in the process of moving in. These new Works will enable us to greatly increase our production and adopt a more progressive policy than in the past.

Enclosed you will find a leaflet giving full particulars of our various models and prices. For the 1928 Season the Standard 12.40 H.P. car will include Four Wheel Brakes at £275 and there will be a still more complete accessory equipment on all Cars.

We are also introducing a 6-cylinder 15.45 H.P. £15 Tax car. The chassis specification is the same as our De Luxe, only 6 inches longer wheel base. This car is to be listed at £425 for 3-seater and 6-seater and £550 for the Saloon, either coach built or fabric.

Should you be contemplating purchasing a new car or an exchange, we would be willing at any time to call upon you for the purpose of giving you the opportunity of inspecting and testing our latest and most successful productions.

Yours faithfully,
HAMPTON CARS (LONDON) LTD.

J. W. Leno
SALES DIRECTOR

THE 12 H.P.
4 CYLINDER
Hampton Car
A
SHORT DESCRIPTION
AND SPECIFICATION
HAMPTON CARS (LONDON) LTD.
DUDBRIDGE, STROUD,
GLOUCESTERSHIRE.

designed not only to contain costs but to give future creditors and customers a little more confidence which must have been at rock bottom by now. Not surprisingly, their work force was reduced considerably during this very difficult period.

So, established in their own works for the first time and with lower overheads, was this the dawn of a new era that could lead to a profitable company at long last ?

Harry Baxter was now chief draughtsman having gained considerable experience working closely with Paddon, Joseph

USEFUL INFORMATION.

		STANDARD	DE LUXE
Weight of Chassis	...	10¾ cwt.	11 cwt.
Weight of two-seater	...	15½ cwt.	16 cwt.
Weight of four-seater	...	16½ cwt.	17 cwt.
Weight of coupe	...	16½ cwt.	17 cwt.
Wheelbase ...	...	8 ft. 9 ins.	9 ft. 2 ins.
Wheel track ...	...	4 ft. 0 ins.	4 ft. 4 ins.
Length and width overall	...	12 ft. x 5 ft.	12 ft. 6 in. x 5 ft.
Petrol capacity	...	7 gallons	7 gallons
Oil capacity ...	...	1 gallon	1 gallon
Water capacity	...	4 gallons	4 gallons
Body space ...	...	7 ft. 7 ins.	8 ft. 2 ins.
Ground clearance	...	9 ins.	9 ins.
Bore ...	...	69 m/m.	69 m/m.
Stroke ...	...	100 m/m.	100 m/m.
Cubic capacity ...	...	1496	1496
R.A.C. rating ...	...	11.9 h.p.	11.9 h.p.
Tax ...	...	£12	£12
Weight in lbs. per c.c. :—			
Two-seater	...	1.16	
Four-seater and coupe		1.23	
Tappet clearance	.	.004 ins.	
Torque ...		67 ft. lbs. at 1500 r.p.m.	

In top gear engine revs. to road speeds at 1000 R.P.M. to 18.5 M.P.H. with 4.5 to 1 back axle ratio.

Third speed ratio	...	6.11 to 1	or	6.86 to 1
Second speed ratio	...	9.32 to 1	or	10.5 to 1
First speed ratio	...	14.85 to 1	or	16.68 to 1

Prices, illustrations and equipment specified in this Booklet are given without engagement, and may be modified without previous notice.

Telegrams—STROUD 271. Telephone No.—STROUD 27

8

Outstanding Features

THE Hampton is a car of all round capabilities. It is built at the foot of the Cotswold Hills, and no finer testing ground could possibly be found.

The aim of the Hampton Designers has been to build a car capable of slow speeds on top gear, and which also combines ease of control in traffic with the ability to climb the steepest hill under full load with ease.

Cheapness in the Hampton sense is cheapness born of excellence. In the long run the Hampton is the cheapest light car on the market because of the high standard to which it is built.

The running and upkeep costs of the Hampton are low, and whilst you have the advantage of possessing a really aristocratic little car that in actual performance gives the greatest measure of service, you are, at the same time, motoring with true economy.

The Hampton coachwork is designed with a real knowledge of what genuine comfort demands. It is roomy, well upholstered, extremely handsome, and provides complete weather protection.

BRITISH BUILT THROUGHOUT.

2

Hampton Cars (London) Ltd. First leaflet.

and Milward since he joined Hamptons in 1920. He was responsible for most of the engineering drawings required which were being revised to reflect the changes now demanded by customers - notably, the 4 wheel braking system with its generous 12 inch drums, the modified transmission and the rear suspension changes.

Still a young man (only 24 in 1928), he was probably very pleased to move his drawing board to the two storey Cotswold stone office block on Selsley Hill because he then lived with his parents in Lower Dudbridge House, only 25 yards away on the other side of the road. Speaking from personal experience, the author is sure that Harry would have welcomed the move to this light and airy environment on Hampton's new site but it is doubtful if the factory workers would have taken the same view of their ex foundry building. Some of Baxter's excellent drawings are illustrated overleaf.

Unfortunately, Hampton had lost touch with many of its traditional customers and dealers by now and only 27 cars were sold in 1928 with seemingly limited prospects for improvement.

In 1928 Milward advertised his first six cylinder engine with a capacity of 1683cc, designated 15/45 with a 63mm bore and 90mm stroke. However, as Meadows did not make an engine to this specification - what was its origin ? There are no records of cars sold with this engine so perhaps it was the stillborn design that was rumoured for in-house production.

The 1.5 litre 12hp model was planned to be the staple product for this period

continued on Page 104

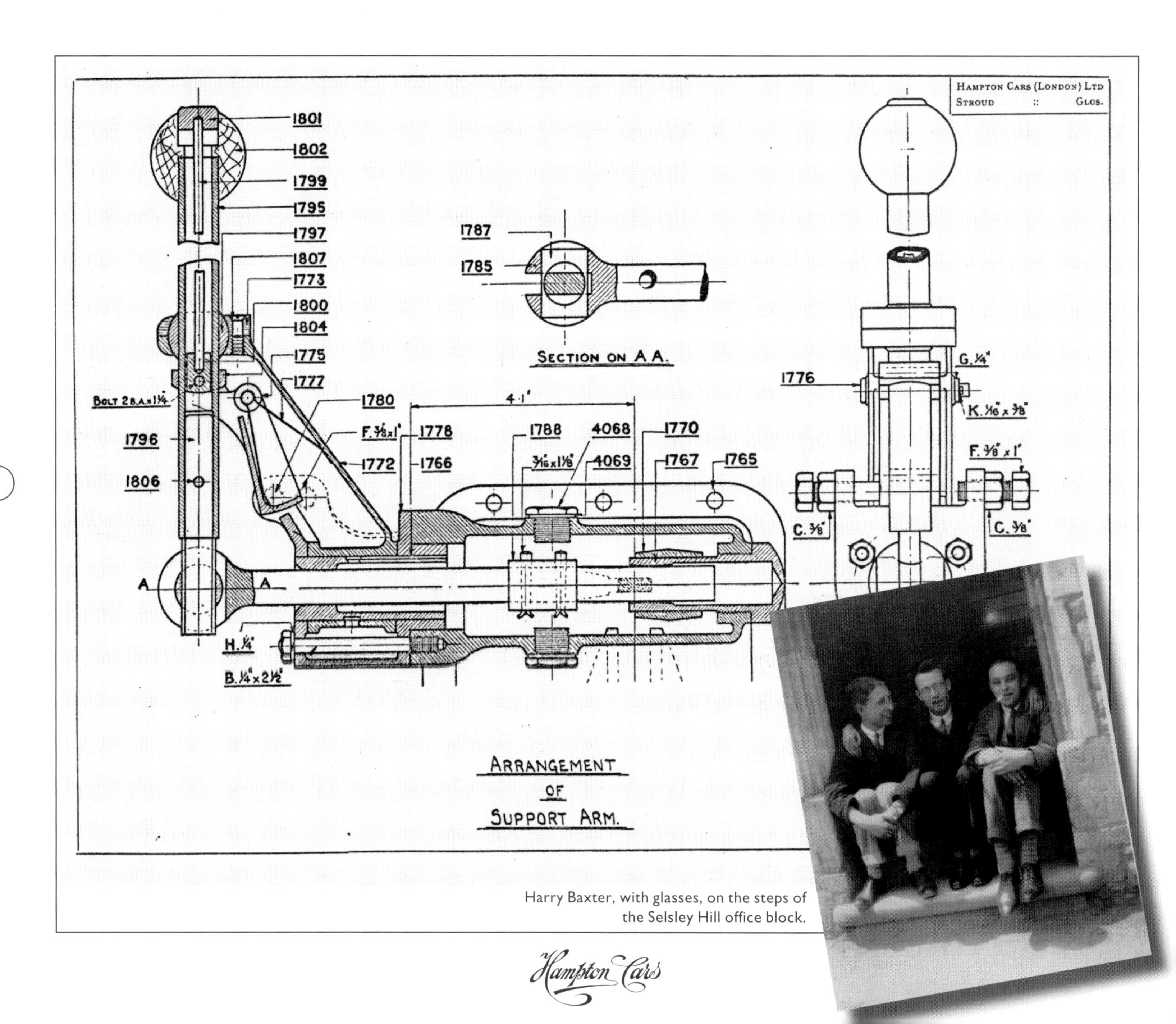

Harry Baxter, with glasses, on the steps of the Selsley Hill office block.

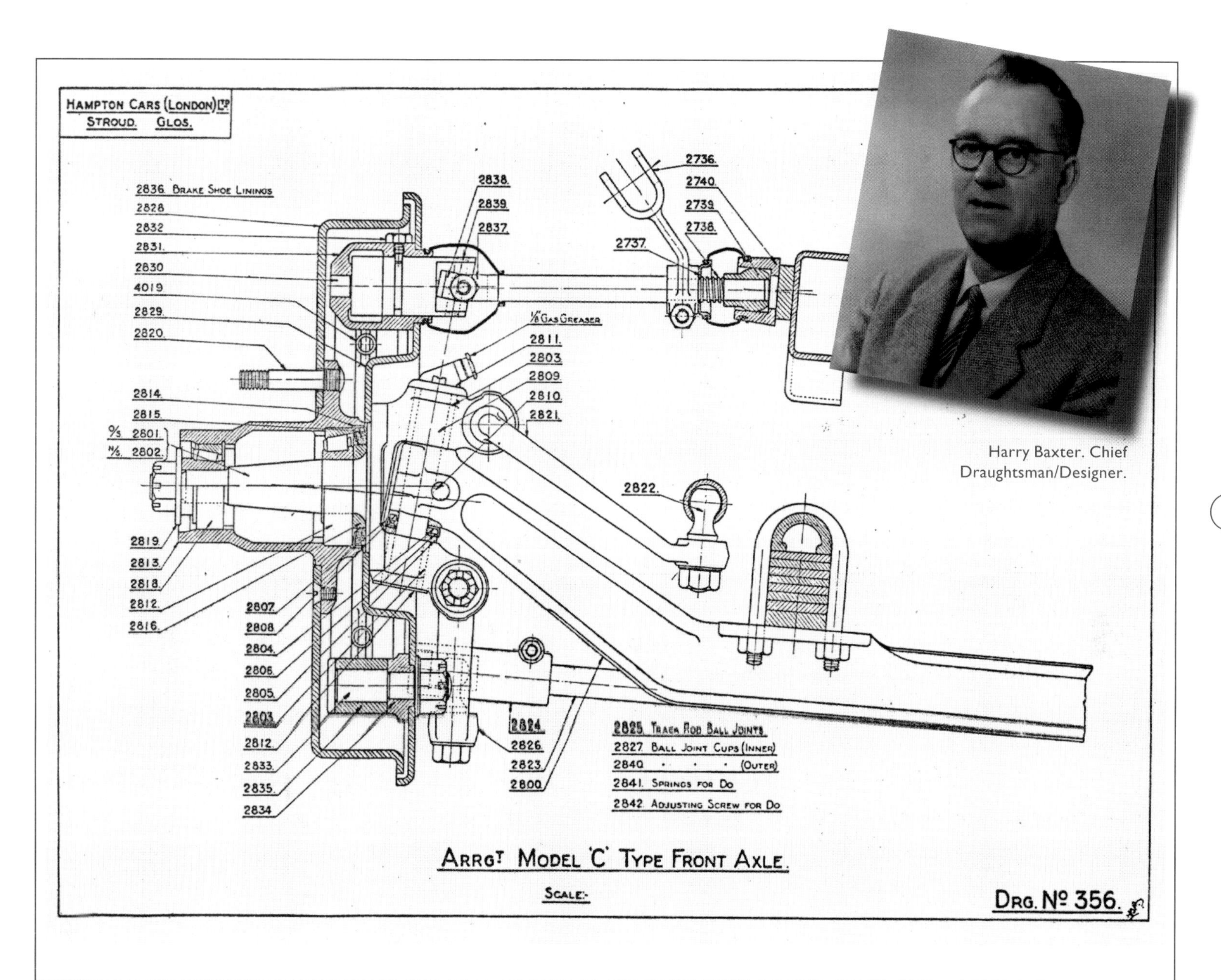

Hampton Cars (London) Ltd
Stroud. Glos.
2836. Brake Shoe Linings
2828
2832
2831.
2830
4019.
2829.
2820.
2814.
2815.
% 2801.
N/S. 2802.
2819.
2813.
2818.
2812.
2816.
2838.
2839.
2837.
1/8 Gas Greaser
2811.
2803.
2809.
2810.
2821.
2736.
2740.
2739.
2738.
2737.
2822.
2807.
2808.
2804.
2806.
2805.
2803.
2812.
2833.
2835.
2834
2824.
2826.
2823.
2800.
2825. Track Rod Ball Joints
2827. Ball Joint Cups (Inner)
2840 " " " (Outer)
2841. Springs for Do
2842. Adjusting Screw for Do
Arrgt Model 'C' Type Front Axle.
Scale:-
Drg. No 356.

Harry Baxter. Chief Draughtsman/Designer.

now referred to as the 12-40 with the Meadows three main bearing engine (designated 4ED).

By the summer of 1929 there was no significant improvement in production or sales even though they had re-introduced their popular 9.8hp economy model with the 1247 cc engine. At this point Milward took another desperate gamble and began work on a much larger car based on a Meadows 6 cylinder 3 litre ohv power plant. Strangely, this engine configuration did not appear in the Meadows standard range shown at the 1928 or 1929 Motor Shows although a unit with the same stroke (120mm) but different bore (69mm) was shown in 1927 with a capacity of 2692cc. The engines purchased by Hampton cars had a bore of 72.5mm, giving a capacity of 2973cc - so was born the 20 hp Hampton. New bodies were designed and produced for the 1929 Olympia Motor Show - both utilising the same chassis. (The bodywork was probably contracted out to H.H. Martyn of Cheltenham as production facilities at Dudbridge were now somewhat limited.) The Empire Saloon was priced at £525. and the Gloster Saloon £495. Hampton also featured a 12hp fabric saloon called The Nailsworth with the 12/40 3 bearing Meadows sports engine at £375. and a 10hp Sportsman Coupé with fabric body at £295. A part of the strong and hard hitting sales literature is reproduced overleaf to allow readers to form their own opinions. This wordy, eight page 11" x 8" three colour brochure was printed by James & Owen Ltd. in their works in Selsley Hill, on the opposite side of the road from Hampton's factory. The Company had booked Stand No. 1 at Olympia and bearing in mind they had been absent for the three previous years, were hopeful of making a big impact. Many of the lavish brochures described above were distributed. One of the 3 litre show cars did eventually sell - the Empire saloon to Mr. George Bord of Whitchurch, Glamorgan. (Reg. No. TX 8828) and a coupé (TX 8981) also found a home in South Wales a little later. Sadly only three other 3 litre cars were sold in 1930. Despite all this activity 1929 was as bad as the previous year with just thiry one cars sold including sixteen 10hp and fourteen 12hp.

The office staff relax on the steps of the office block. "Pops" Joel (left), Milward's secretary, Dene Webb (right), Leno's secretary and Harry Baxter in centre.

By early 1930 prospects were once again grim with only a trickle of cars leaving the works - just twenty three small models and the four 3 litre cars. Their impressive display at the London Show had been a failure and had not generated the expected sales. By spring 1930 cash was again running out and

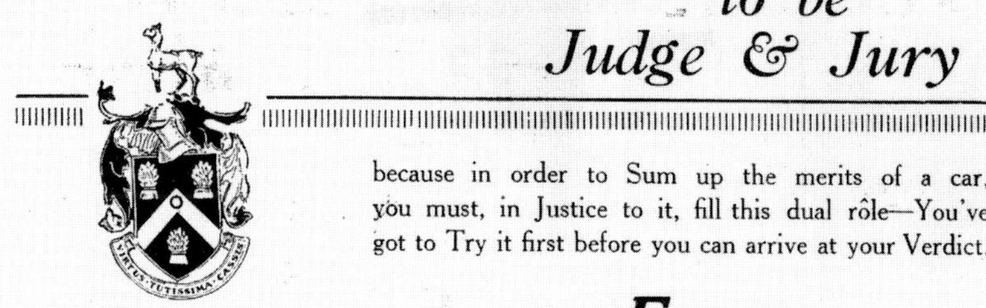

We Want You
to be
Judge & Jury
because in order to Sum up the merits of a car, you must, in Justice to it, fill this dual rôle—You've got to Try it first before you can arrive at your Verdict.
The EMPIRE "SIX"
3-Litre Hampton
strikes a new note in the British motoring world. It is our firm Conviction that its many outstanding qualities will acclaim it
THE SENSATION OF THE YEAR IN CAR CIRCLES
and so satisfied are we with its performance and value that we extend to you a cordial invitation to Try it—the acid test of merit—and Judge for yourself.
Your Verdict, we are confident, will be unanimous and one over which we can justly enthuse.
SEE IT ON
Stand No. 1
OLYMPIA
Price £495
AND ARRANGE A TRIAL. REMEMBER—THE HAMPTON IS THE ONLY ALL-BRITISH 3-LITRE "SIX" on the market at AN ECONOMIC FIGURE.
See also other models
9 h.p. Fabric Saloon £295
12/40 h.p. models from £315
Distributors for London and South:
AYLESBURY MOTOR CO. LTD., 136, Great Portland Street, W.1, and Aylesbury, Bucks.
C. B. WARDMAN .. 198, Great Portland Street, W.1.
Distributors for Scotland:
M. MACINTYRE LTD. .. 130, Renfrew Street, GLASGOW.
Distributors for Cardiff and District:
PARSONS MOTORS LTD. .. Westgate Street, CARDIFF.
HAMPTON CARS (London) LTD., STROUD, GLOS.

Advertisement in The Autocar 18 Oct. 1929

Hampton's distribution network appeared to be down to just three, namely: Aylesbury Motor Co. Ltd, Great Portland Street, London. M. Macintyre Ltd., Renfrew Street, Glasgow. Parsons Motors Ltd. Cardiff.

It seems that at long last their most loyal and long serving dealer, B.S. Marshall from London, had thrown in the towel, as had The Neath & District Automobile Co. Ltd. (David T. Jones). It is most regrettable that the Companies House records covering these years were destroyed in 1962 and particularly those relating to the early 1930's so the extent of their financial problems cannot be measured. John Hatton-Hall and his reluctant colleagues, Milward and Leno, had no alternative at this stage but to call it a day. After all, only 132 cars were produced in over four years of their ownership - the lowest output of any of the regimes. The selection of Thomas Godman as Receiver is intriguing. He was not a qualified accountant but as he had recently come to live just round the corner from the Hampton Works at the elegant Cainscross House, his travelling expenses would be low. He took office on 9th July 1930 and proceeded to make arrangements to wind up the Company and dispose of the assets of which the only significant one was their freehold factory and office block in Selsley Hill. Interestingly, Godman also had a small London office in Woburn Place which indicates that perhaps he was a friend or at least known to John Hatton-Hall. John Leno left without delay but Milward stayed on for a period to help oversee the liquidation, perhaps feeling he still had a part to play in conducting the last rites of Hampton Cars.

The Hampton

3 LITRE

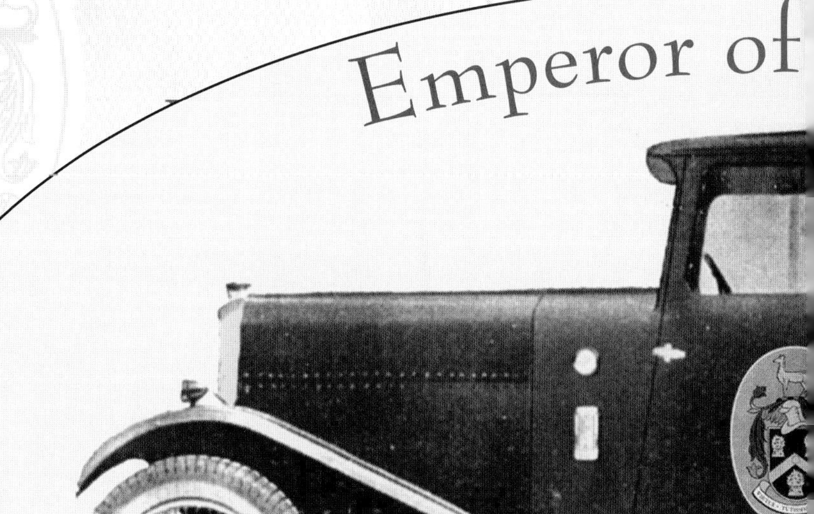

DESPITE the steadily increasing popularity constantly asked by many of our own possible value and performance.

So persistent has been this call from home a exhaustive tests we are now introducing our

"EMPIRE" 6 Cylin

With the knowledge of the public requirements it production, which incorporates the following features :—

1.—The flexibility of the big six.

2.—The speed of the best sports car.

3.—An astounding top gear performance.

4.—Acceleration which is generally supposed to be the absolute preogative o

5.—At a price never before attempted in the British car market.

In this All British production, the power unit is by Messrs. Henry Meadows, Ltd., of Wolverhampton and is without doubt the most wonderful achievement of this up-to-date and most progressive firm. Apart from the power unit the remainder of the Chassis is built at our Stroud Works and follows orthodox lines adopted by us out of our 17 years past experience of Hampton Car construction.

The Chassis has a 10 foot wheelbase, and 4ft. 8 in. track, sufficiently large to accommodate

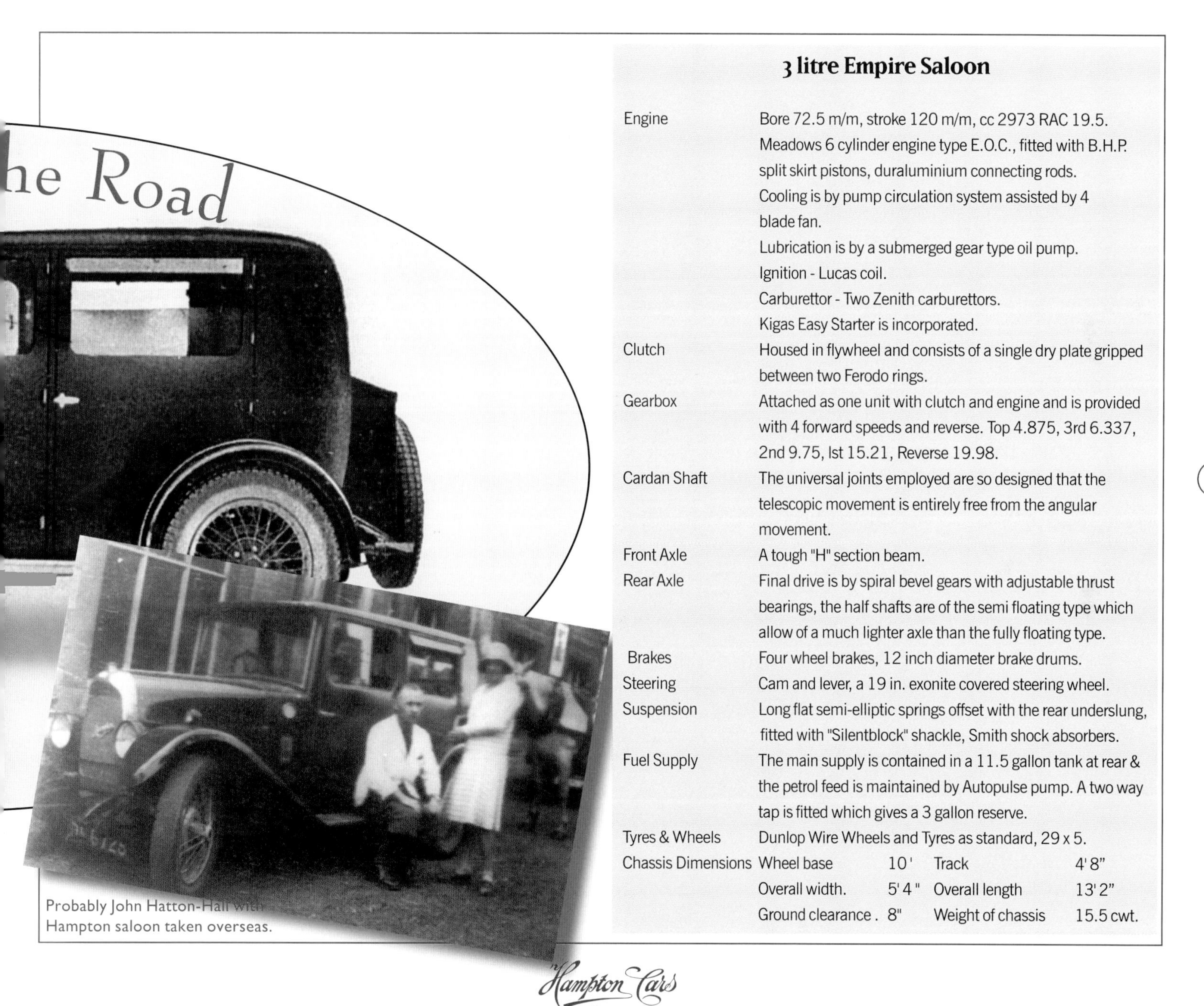

Probably John Hatton-Hall with Hampton saloon taken overseas.

3 litre Empire Saloon

Engine	Bore 72.5 m/m, stroke 120 m/m, cc 2973 RAC 19.5. Meadows 6 cylinder engine type E.O.C., fitted with B.H.P. split skirt pistons, duraluminium connecting rods. Cooling is by pump circulation system assisted by 4 blade fan. Lubrication is by a submerged gear type oil pump. Ignition - Lucas coil. Carburettor - Two Zenith carburettors. Kigas Easy Starter is incorporated.
Clutch	Housed in flywheel and consists of a single dry plate gripped between two Ferodo rings.
Gearbox	Attached as one unit with clutch and engine and is provided with 4 forward speeds and reverse. Top 4.875, 3rd 6.337, 2nd 9.75, lst 15.21, Reverse 19.98.
Cardan Shaft	The universal joints employed are so designed that the telescopic movement is entirely free from the angular movement.
Front Axle	A tough "H" section beam.
Rear Axle	Final drive is by spiral bevel gears with adjustable thrust bearings, the half shafts are of the semi floating type which allow of a much lighter axle than the fully floating type.
Brakes	Four wheel brakes, 12 inch diameter brake drums.
Steering	Cam and lever, a 19 in. exonite covered steering wheel.
Suspension	Long flat semi-elliptic springs offset with the rear underslung, fitted with "Silentblock" shackle, Smith shock absorbers.
Fuel Supply	The main supply is contained in a 11.5 gallon tank at rear & the petrol feed is maintained by Autopulse pump. A two way tap is fitted which gives a 3 gallon reserve.
Tyres & Wheels	Dunlop Wire Wheels and Tyres as standard, 29 x 5.

Chassis Dimensions				
	Wheel base	10'	Track	4' 8"
	Overall width.	5' 4"	Overall length	13' 2"
	Ground clearance .	8"	Weight of chassis	15.5 cwt.

8

The Famous Five -
The survivors examined

The survival rate of Hampton Cars is disappointingly low and for this reason a detailed examination of our famous five - the survivors - is considered essential. Of course, if we include the Motor Cycle, there are actually six Hampton products still with us but - consistent with our subject title - we shall concentrate on the five remaining cars.

In many ways HT 1526 is our most important survivor even though at the present time it is in a dismantled state undergoing restoration . Why important ? Mainly because if Max Williamson had not been stimulated by this particular Hampton he would probably not have taken such an active interest in the history of the marque. It is the only survivor from the original Dudbridge company, the only one with a Dorman engine and the only example of what is essentially the pre-War design, incorporating the remote gearbox and 3/4 elliptic rear suspension.

HT 1526

ENGINEERING COY LTD
Hampton
STROUD ENGLAND

Hobbs Brothers Yard - 1948. Driver Ken Hobbs, Front seat - Geoff Browning. Others left to right: Tanker driver, Bob Jordon, Harry Brown, John Turner, Frank Cook.

The chassis frame is reasonably conventional with five cross members and a lowered longitudinal section - or sub-frame - which supports the engine and remote gearbox. This contrasts with the simplified later design (1922/23) for the Meadows-engined cars which had only three cross members between more substantial chassis rails - to which the engine/gearbox unit was directly attached.

Most of the 1920 cars had the smaller 63mm x 120mm Dorman engines but this example is one of the twenty four with the 69mm x 120mm larger engine, some component parts of which are illustrated. The one-piece crankcase and engine block are made of aluminium with pressed-in cast iron wet liners forming the cylinders.

Chain driven twin camshafts operate the inclined overhead valves through external push rods on each side of the engine and the cylinder head would be described today as cross-flow with inlet on one side and exhaust on the other.

The two-bearing crankshaft is supported by a long white metal bearing at the rear with a large diameter self-aligning ball-bearing at the front. The con rods pick up their lubrication from troughs fed with oil by a pressure pump, whilst the rockers are fed through an oil bearing wick.

Power is transmitted to the three speed gearbox through a leather faced cone clutch and short shaft with disc-and-spider

universal joints. The gearbox has right hand change which was normal in this period. The rear axle is of built-up construction and designed so that the half shafts can be removed while the car still rests on its wheels. The brakes are arranged side by side within each drum - foot brake operating one pair of shoes and hand brake the other.

There are no front brakes; again, normal for this time. The road wheels are of Sankey manufacture and are fitted with 710 x 90 beaded edge tyres.

The 24 page handbook for this model gives further information presented in a friendly, non-technical manner. It seems that the task of educating motorists in the Twenties was an integral part of selling motor vehicles.

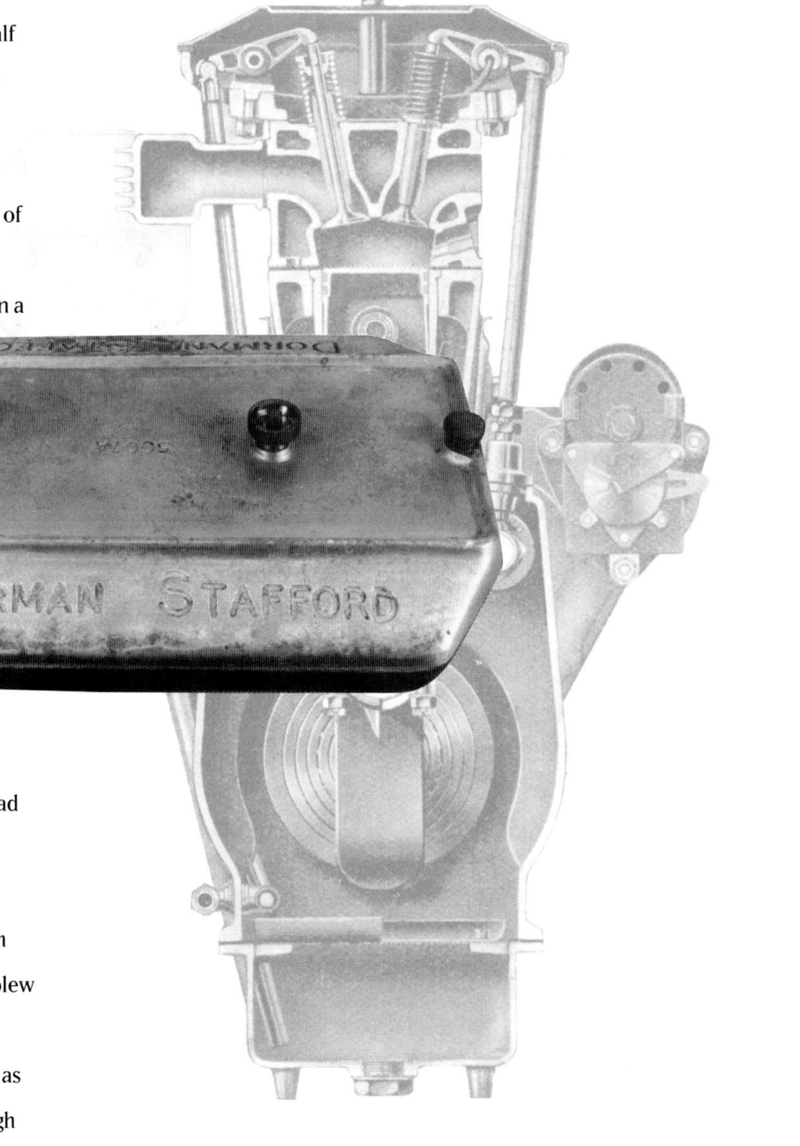

Rocker Cover

HT 1526 was supplied new in September 1920 to a Mr. A.F. Coates of The Imperial Tobacco Company, Bristol. Research has not revealed how long Mr. Coates kept the car but it spent the next ten years mostly in the Dorset area and returned to Stroud in 1931. It was then in the ownership of Mr. B.J. Asher of Victoria Villas, Whiteshill - some three miles from where it had been built - and was last licensed for use on the road in 1936.

It re-emerged in 1948 when it was discovered by local businessman and motoring enthusiast, Ken Hobbs, in Wiggall's scrap yard just 200 yards from the original Dudbridge Hampton factory. He "put some petrol in the tank, blew up the tyres" and drove it half a mile up the road to his Cashes Green yard where it remained until 1953. Max and a friend, Pat Birt, bought it from him as a joint restoration project and moved it to Bert Walter's farm at Rodborough

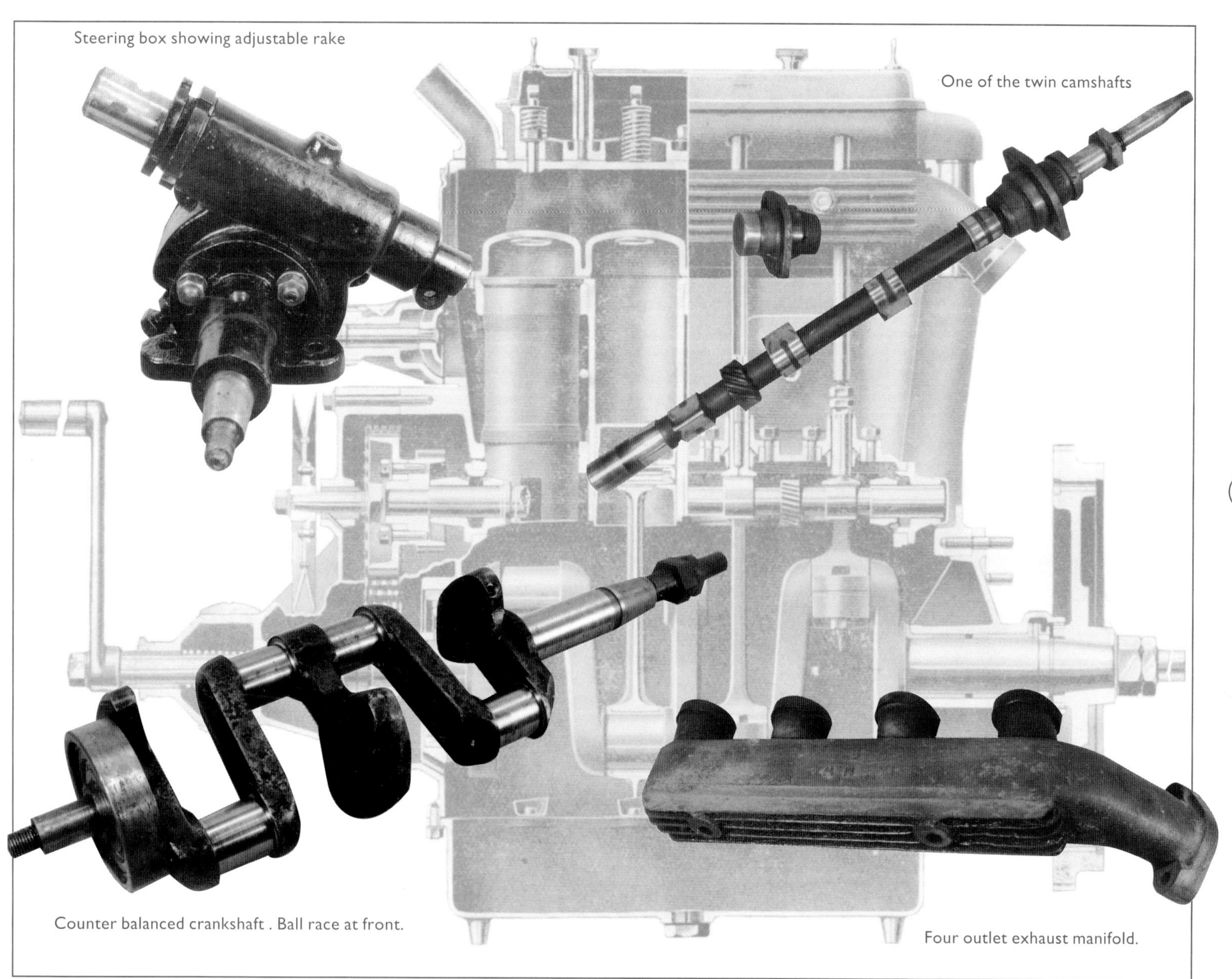

Steering box showing adjustable rake

One of the twin camshafts

Counter balanced crankshaft . Ball race at front.

Four outlet exhaust manifold.

Rear brake drum & axle showing dual brake shoes.

where the new owners soon had it running round the farmer's field.

The 1927 Austin 12/4 saloon (**YC 662**) seen towing **HT 1526** to its new home was owned by a Dutchman, Leo van-der-Waals, who was a friend of Pat Birt. This car has recently emerged from over 30 years storage and was sold at a local auction so is likely to be restored. Perhaps the Hampton and the Austin will meet again in the not too distant future, this time travelling under their own steam.

Bronze wheel hubs.

A little later Max became the sole owner of the Hampton. In Pat's own words "Max had rather different views from me regarding how one sets about re-building a car so he bought me out very early on" - the consideration being in the order of £10. Fortunately, despite the passage of 43 years, Pat - now the Rev. Pat Birt, Vicar of Stour Provost in Dorset - has been been able to provide useful information about **HT 1526** to add to our story.

The car languished in a garage at the Royal William, Cranham (between Stroud and Cheltenham) for a period in the late Fifties and lost a few of its external fittings. However, most of them were proprietary items and replacements have since been located. The photographs show some of its interesting component parts, some castings sporting their Hampton logos.

HT 1526 being towed from Ken Hobbs' yard in 1953.

Useful Hints FOR THE Care & Maintenance OF THE HAMPTON CAR.

Hampton Engineering Com[pany]
(1920) Limited
Works: DUDBRIDGE, near St[roud]
GLOS.
Telephone: Stroud 271, 272.

YC 662 in 1997.

14

CLUTCH.

The Clutch is of the Cone leather-to-metal type. The cone itself is lined with a band of leather under which are a number of small flat springs placed at intervals round the cone to ensure a smooth and gradual take up when the clutch is being engaged.

TO ADJUST THE CLUTCH. At the rear of the cone three adjusting screws are provided which, when screwed in or out, increase or decrease the tension of the clutch spring. Thus, should the Clutch be too fierce, it is only necessary to unscrew the adjusting screws sufficiently until the clutch engages smoothly without unnecessary snatching.

The flywheel boss is turned down to carry a ball-race which is held in position by the Clutch Spring. This ball-race only comes into operation when the engine is running and the clutch has been disengaged, but it should be frequently lubricated to prevent it seizing up.

The drive from the clutch to the gear box is taken up by an internal and external gear coupling, as shown in Fig. 1, and a universal joint in front of the gear box.

FIG. 1.

SECTIONAL ARRANGEMENT OF CLUTCH

CLUTCH ACTION.—The Clutch Pedal is connected to the pedal crossbar, and when the former is depressed the clutch release ring, which rests in the Clutch Fork, is carried forward and bears against a flange on the clutch centre, thus pushing the clutch cone forward and disengaging it from the clutch flange.

On releasing the pedal the spring carries the clutch back into the original position.

By reference to Fig. 1 this action will be quite understood.

15

The Clutch Release Ring should always be well supplied with grease in the cup provided.

TO DISMANTLE THE CLUTCH.—First disconnect the universal joint in front of the gear box and remove the clutch centre shaft. Next, lower the brackets which hold the pedal cross-bar, so that when the clutch flange is finally released from the engine flywheel the whole can be lifted clear. Care should be taken to see that the steel balls in the bearing on the flywheel are not lost, as the bearing is a loose one. Before reassembling well grease the continuation of the crankshaft and the ball bearing.

See that the spring is properly over the bush at the rear of the flywheel.

TRANSMISSION.—This is of the usual gear box type, having three forward speeds and one reverse; normally this requires no attention other than lubrication (see Lubrication). Fig. 2 will give an idea of the construction of the gear box.

From the gear box the transmission is carried to the back axle by the main driving shaft connected at either end by very strong fibre disc joints.

FIG. 2.

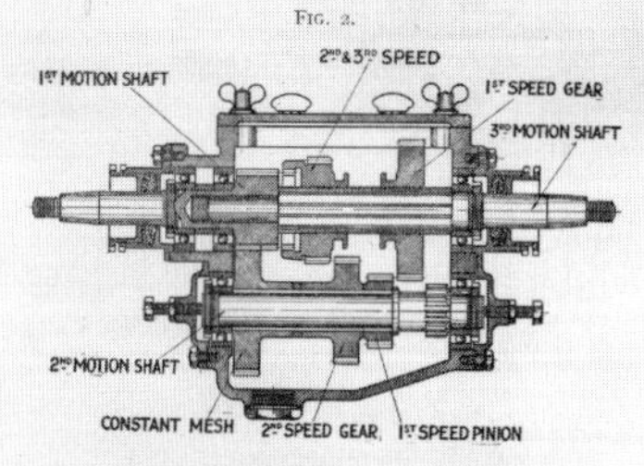

SECTIONAL ARRANGEMENT OF GEAR BOX

Keith Stimson with his Hampton radiator.

When the restored vehicle arrives on the vintage car scene it will undoubtedly create interest particularly as it embodies many features from Paddon's pre-War design, including the dropped sub-frame, the rear axle, remote 3 speed gear box and the rear suspension.

Gearbox supported on longitudinal sub frame.

Chassis with 3/4 elliptic rear suspension.

Minnie Hampton was the nickname given to **HN 4091** when it was first re-discovered by the late Alastair Monro, Bonnie's brother. Reference to the photograph shows the much reduced wheelbase. Mike Worthington-Williams, the well known motoring historian, who has always carried a torch for Hampton cars, reported in Old Motor in December 1981 the details of how Alastair found the car in Yorkshire and took it home to Leatherhead with a view to restoration. This car was built by The Stroud Motor Manufacturing Co. and although it had previously been designated a 1924 model by both Bonnie and Mike, the chassis number 2665 indicates that it was manufactured in 1925. This is substantiated by the fact that its 12hp Meadows engine arrived at the factory in May 1925. The car is a T10 model (as indicated by its body plate) which were normally only advertised with the smaller 10hp unit. However, as it is known that at least two other T10 Hamptons were supplied around this period with the larger engine, this supports the view that this engine is the original one fitted by the factory.

The external dimensions of both engines were identical so no engineering adjustments would have been necessary. The car was originally built as a four seater open tourer but William Longstaff, the previous owner, had purchased it just after the War with only 5,000 miles on the clock; he removed the body and modified the chassis to take a Morris Cowley rear axle as he had experienced problems with a worn bearing on the original axle. All this butchery was carried out to enable him to use the Hampton for towing his grass cutting machinery round his farm - wearing out first gear but little else.

After its grass cutting days it lay idle for nine years but fortunately when discovered in 1978 many of the discarded parts, including the original rear axle, windscreen and brake parts, were found nearby and loaded onto the trailer.

Just three years later, sadly, Alastair died and his widow, Mary, passed the car on to his sister, Bonnie. Whilst being grateful for the gesture she felt unable to cope with another Hampton and its restoration so the car was sold in 1982 to a Stroud motor enthusiast, Nigel Brown.

Nigel had several other cars including a Dellow and an Allard but owing to pressure of business he only made limited progress towards the substantial re-build that **HN 4091** needed. In 1995 a career change necessitated a move to Staffordshire so the Hampton stayed in the Stroud area with a new owner, Fraser Partridge, who is now actively working on its restoration. The original axle and braking system have been re-fitted after extensive repair to the rear of the chassis frame, severely damaged when the Morris suspension was substituted. The vehicle is now a running chassis complete with bulkhead, screen, fuel tank and a full set of dash panel

instruments. Take note of an interesting design feature concerning the special fuel filler which doubles as a spout when attached to a standard two gallon can which were popular in the Twenties.

The Meadows engine has a neat four port fluted exhaust manifold and many of the castings show the Hampton script, giving a good cohesive feel to the design. Evidence of Albert Moores' fine patternmaking skills can again be seen on the castings, the rear axle differential unit, the clutch and gearbox covers and the engine side plates. This car still features the adjustable steering rake, rear wheel brakes only and the central accelerator pedal. This is the only T10 model to survive out of around 386 produced.

The next major project is to create a new body which is under detailed consideration. The car was last used on public roads in 1933 but with most of the basic mechanical work now completed by Fraser perhaps the day is not too far away when he can drive it the four miles from Thrupp down to the original works at Dudbridge where it was built. We wish him luck.

Alastair Monro surveys his "Minnie Hampton" ready for its journey to Leatherhead, 1981.

Braking system. Note adjustment wing nuts.

The front wheel hub.

HN 4091 Body plate.

The dual purpose fuel cap.

The Meadows 12hp engine - 4EC two main bearings.

Instrument panel.

Hampton clutch and gearbox covers.

Examination of almost any vintage car encyclopaedia or illustrated reference book produced during the last 35 years that contains details of Hampton cars will probably contain a photograph of HW 2734. Most surprisingly this high profile car is frequently referred to as a 1927 model which is the year the owner Bonnie Monro genuinely believed it was produced, influenced firstly by Mr. Hobson, a pawnbroker from Bristol, the original owner of the car. He had previously been the owner of a 1921 open 4 seater Hampton tourer and claimed that HW 2734 had been built to his own specification in 1926 ! It is more likely that he really meant that he had specified certain factory fitted extras not usually part of the standard two seater coupé, namely wire wheels, tubular front and rear bumpers, Triplex safety glass etc. Much later, when Bonnie showed the retired John Leno her car, he thought that it was of 1927 vintage which pleased and excited Bonnie as she was born in the same year in Hampton in Middlesex.

However, reference to the chassis and engine numbers and the original log book indicates the car was produced in the middle of 1928. Both the body identification plate and a threshold plate under the driver's door reveal that it was a product of Hampton Cars (London) Ltd. - the last significant Hampton manufacturer.

Previous owners included Mark Stent in Surrey and W.A. Stone in Sussex, before it was spotted by Michael Sedgwick who suggested it would be a good restoration project for Peter Moseley. Peter sympathetically restored it in the late Fifties and eventually entered it in the Second Beaulieu Auction in 1961. A 34 year old Bonnie, without a driving licence, successfully bid £62.10.0. to become its owner and triggered a new era in her life. This car exudes originality which results from Bonnie's philosophy of not being tempted into expensive cosmetic restoration. The seats, for example, are well worn; the door handles and knobs are correct; the Auster opening windscreen has all the proper period fittings. A sliding brass ventilator is fitted into the front of the hood frame which also has two neat cam operated levers to locate the hood positively on the protruding frame spigots. The Lucas vacuum headlight dipping system and air operated screen wiper are both interesting features. The oval dash panel contains speedometer/ammeter/oil pressure gauge/clock and switches. Clustered around the steering column are the headlight dipping knob, the starter button and a Hobson telegauge fuel gauge (not working). A wire choke cable and a motor cycle style lever appear to be the only non-original fittings. The ratchet type wind up windows with hinged supporting channel are something of a luxury particularly when compared with peg type side screens fitted to some other contemporary vehicles. Any paintwork needing attention was regularly brush

painted by Bonnie and her sister, Jean. In the early days her brother, Alastair helped her with mechanical work and later she struck up a good working relationship with the veteran ex-Brooklands engineer, John Granville Grenfell, whose depth of knowledge was ideal to help her to keep this particular car in good running order.

Her mother showed an active interest in the car and was frequently seen as a passenger and co-performer at summer shows. She had a passion for seeking out any parts of the car manufactured from brass and polishing them regularly as if she had shares in "Brasso". In reality the brightwork would originally have been nickel plated (by The Stroud Metal Company - Hampton's old associates). Bonnie visited Stroud on several occasions including a special invitation to display her car at the 1966 Stroud Show. Naturally, she made friends with several of Hampton's former employees, many of whom regularly corresponded with her. On one of these visits Mr. and Mrs. Harold Harmer, then of Belmont Road, presented her with a toasting fork made from Hampton car parts as Harold was the spares man at the works. Surprisingly, this fork has survived the passage of time, having been found recently at the bottom of a box of Hampton spares. According to Harold the brass handle was a bonnet clip, the shaft a copper carburettor pipe and the prongs were made from the gear lever trigger rod. In his later years he became well known as a hairdresser in Nailsworth and his wife ran whist drives for the Red Cross. Harold also sent a photograph of a Leyland lorry being used for six weeks to provide power to Hampton's machine shop during coal strikes in the early Twenties. (See Page 56) The exhaust fumes did create some initial problems but an elaborate system of ducting eventually avoided serious carbon monoxide poisoning amongst the workers. The modern day Health & Safety

Mr. Hobson - the original owner in 1928.

Taken at Badminton Park 1924 - Mr. Hobson seated in the rear of his first 1921 Hampton.

HW 2734 at Peter Moseley's garage, Horsham.

Officer would certainly have had a field day with this situation. What is without question is that the Monro family kept the Hampton name alive for over 30 years and hopefully this will inspire the owners of our survivors to complete their cars and have as much enjoyment as Bonnie had in her unique Hampton.It seems appropriate at this point to hand over some of the story telling to Bonnie herself by reproducing part of her text.

The Pride and Joy of a Vintage Car

By Bonnie Monro

Starting Up. *June 17th, 1961 was the day I "accidentally" became the owner of a rare vintage car, a 1927 Hampton. I went, purely as a spectator, to the Beaulieu Auction and while wandering round the various vintage models, somehow I kept returning to one car which seemed to me to be full of character! When this car - Lot 23 - came under the hammer, I simply couldn't resist it, even though I could not drive. With my brother Alastair's help, I put in a bid and as the bidding progressed, I became more and more determined to have the car, and more and more excited. Then, suddenly, the Hampton was mine - almost by accident! It cost £5 more than my limit, (£62.50 according to a contemporary record) which Alastair added. I could not believe my luck. I felt like jumping for joy. It was at this point, wondering where to put it in safety, that Michael Sedgwick offered to keep it at his home for the night, until we could collect the car the following day to drive*

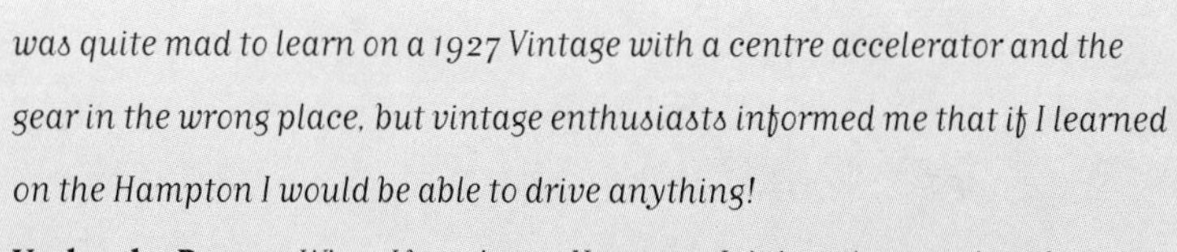

Note the twin bumpers and the step to aid access to the dickey seat.

it one hundred miles back to Weybridge. From that time on Michael always showed great interest in my car.

I had to wait until the following day before we could drive it home. I always said I would have to own a car before I learned to drive, but little dreamt it would be a vintage one. Learning to drive was great fun and probably taught me more about the car itself that any books or demonstrations could have done. Modern car owners seem to think I was quite mad to learn on a 1927 Vintage with a centre accelerator and the gear in the wrong place, but vintage enthusiasts informed me that if I learned on the Hampton I would be able to drive anything!

Under the Bonnet *When I bought my Hampton I did not have a clue about things "under the bonnet". Little by little I began to learn, and then joined the local evening class on Motor Mechanics at the Brooklands Technical College, Weybridge, in Surrey, not far from where I used to live. For the first two terms there were lectures and instructions on taking various spare parts to pieces -*

No. 23 sold - Beaulieu 17th June 1961.

Steering wheel with horn ring.

Dashboard layout

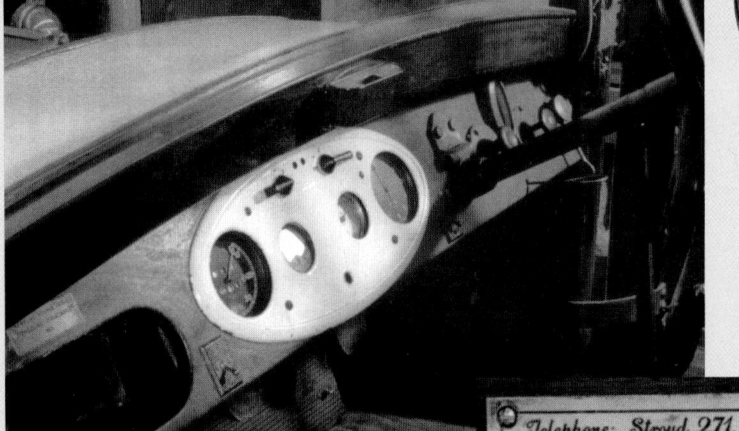

starter motors, dynamos, and carburettors, for instance - and of course hopefully learning to put them together without any pieces left over. It certainly gave me more confidence to gain some knowledge and was very useful. During the Summer term everyone took his or her own car to work on - adjusting tappets, balancing wheels, oiling and greasing correctly, fitting new carbon brushes on the dynamo, were just a few of the jobs tackled.

The petrol tank, which is housed under the bonnet, holds seven gallons. Onlookers are often astonished to see it situated so close to the engine. Having no petrol gauge it was often difficult to judge the amount. By using a solid wooden 12 inch ruler I discovered by trial and error that approximately $1.{}^{3}/_{10}$" equals a gallon - when on the level. In 1967 when parked on Rodborough Common, near Stroud, on seeing me check with this method, a kind fellow

The door furniture.

Threshold plate

presented me with a Brewers Measure made of solid brass. It was then possible to calculate the depth of the petrol in Hogsheads and Firkins! This has caused some amusement over the years.

The Hampton does not possess a fan to cool the engine and in spite of the radiator holding four gallons of water, a traffic jam or slow crawl can be quite a worry. In the early days I attended almost every Rally or Carnival that could be found. Sometimes we were stuck behind a marching band - lovely to hear but agonising to follow as the car grew hotter and HOTTER ! Mind you, a hot engine can have advantages. On one of the Annual Daffodil Runs to

Bournemouth in April organised by the Bean Car Club, I cooked our home-made pies wrapped in foil on top of the rocker box. Out of the blue came a request for the Hampton to take part in a film, in a garage scene at the old Ascot (Berks.) Police Station. The old fashioned buildings were ideal for the setting. It was a bitterly cold day near Christmas when usually the Hampton is tucked up for the winter. The fee offered for one day's filming covered the cost of the licence and the new hood.

In 1971 there was another occasion with other rare Vintage Car Owners to take part, dressed in my 1927 costume with the Hampton in the BBC. documentary film at Bayham Abbey, the seat of the Marquis of Camden. Later we had the added pleasure of watching the result on television.

Fire Away One summer's day in 1963 the Hampton was parked in our driveway in front of the house. Starting up, imagine my horror to see flames from the engine reflected in the brass headlamps. Hastily I threw an old coat over the engine to try and prevent the flames reaching the petrol tank which is housed under the bonnet. As luck would have it, that caught fire too! Reluctantly I grabbed some sand from a heap beside the rockery but apparently it had peat in it and added to the confusion. (It certainly taught me a lesson discovering there was no fire extinguisher to hand and, being wise after the event, was one of the first things to buy). The rest of the family was

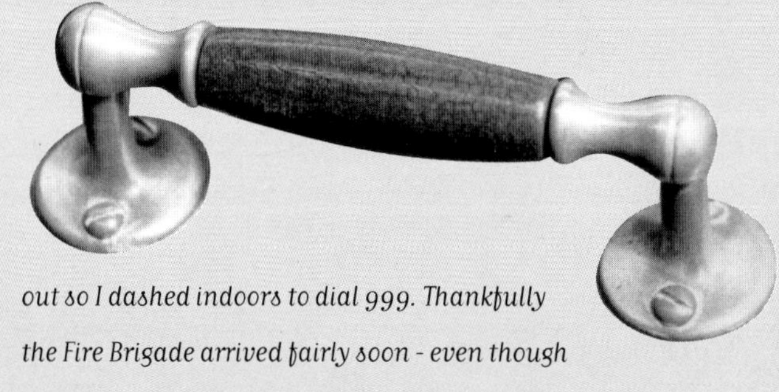

out so I dashed indoors to dial 999. Thankfully the Fire Brigade arrived fairly soon - even though every minute whilst waiting seemed like an hour. The fireman came running down our driveway with a huge hose and then discovered an extinguisher might help. Several squirts of this soon doused the fire and the flames died down just in time. I had visions of the whole car being blown to smithereens, let alone the house ! It was astounding to find, after thoroughly cleaning the engine, that the car started up willingly. After this traumatic occasion I removed the carburettor to have it checked and restored at Solex. The "mature" foreman obviously belonged to the right era and was so fascinated by this section of the car that when I went to collect it he did not charge me a

Michael Sedgwick with Bonnie and Helen Marshall.

penny and it was all clean and polished. Doesn't it renew one's faith in human nature! In 1964 I was invited to enter the Car and Costume event at a Bean Car Club July Rally. I borrowed a genuine 1927 dress and had already been given a hat to go with it. It was fun when my father, acting as doctor, and I won a prize - I think it was the only time he drove the Hampton though over the years he had driven various makes of cars. The following year I made an outfit each for my mother and myself to tone with the colour of the car, black and cream. With suitable hats, drop earrings, long strings of beads and the right period handbags and shoes, we entered another Car and Costume event and were thrilled to win first prize. Whenever we drove round the arena my mother would always receive a huge cheer when she peered at the crowd with her lorgnettes which hung from a black ribbon round her neck. I had a very long cigarette holder, typical of the era, though being a non-smoker I always forgot to take a cigarette. Nine times out of ten, to enter into the spirit of the event, a spectator would lend me one.

The Hampton toasting fork.

Bonnie and Marjorie winning another Car and Costume award. Littlewick Show August 1973.

Without doubt the Hampton gives me more fun, enjoyment and interest than anything I could have owned. Over the years many people have helped me either with advice or practical help or have been willing to search out details of the history. Some problems have been a challenge but the joy and pleasure I've had far outweigh these and it is great to receive a smile and a cheery wave whenever the Hampton and I go out for a drive.

Holey, Holey, Holey ! By Bonnie Monro

Funny things gaskets - always full of hole.
You wouldn't think they'd be much use
To any living soul.
Well, they aren't really - but to a car
That's different, by far.
For keeping oil and water in,
Or out - depending which !
You hope they do the job so well
You never have a hitch.
Paper one, cork ones,
Asbestos lined with copper.
You tighten nuts correctly
And hope they act like a stopper
But if you have a leak,
Then you grumble and you curse;
You poke about to have a look
Making matters worse.
The remedy is simple:
Remove, re-cut, renew it.
As long as you can find the shape,
It's easy when you do it.

This evolved after I had cut and renewed various gaskets in 1972.

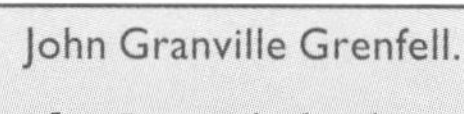
John Granville Grenfell.

After Bonnie's death in 1993 the car passed to her cousin, Mr. Derek Tyler of Kings Lynn who used it on a few occasions before his untimely death in 1996. The Hampton was left to his widow, Dr. Judith Tyler. By this time HW 2734 was showing signs of old age and was in need of maintenance and restoration. However, it put in a most welcome appearance at the opening of Sainsbury's Dudbridge Store on the 5th of March 1997, by kind permission of Dr. Tyler. A couple of months later the author was fortunate to purchase the Hampton and on 26th May it returned to Gloucestershire where it will receive the attention it needs and deserves. This Hampton is home at last - 31 years since it appeared in the Stroud Show Procession and 69 years since it was built in the Hampton Factory.

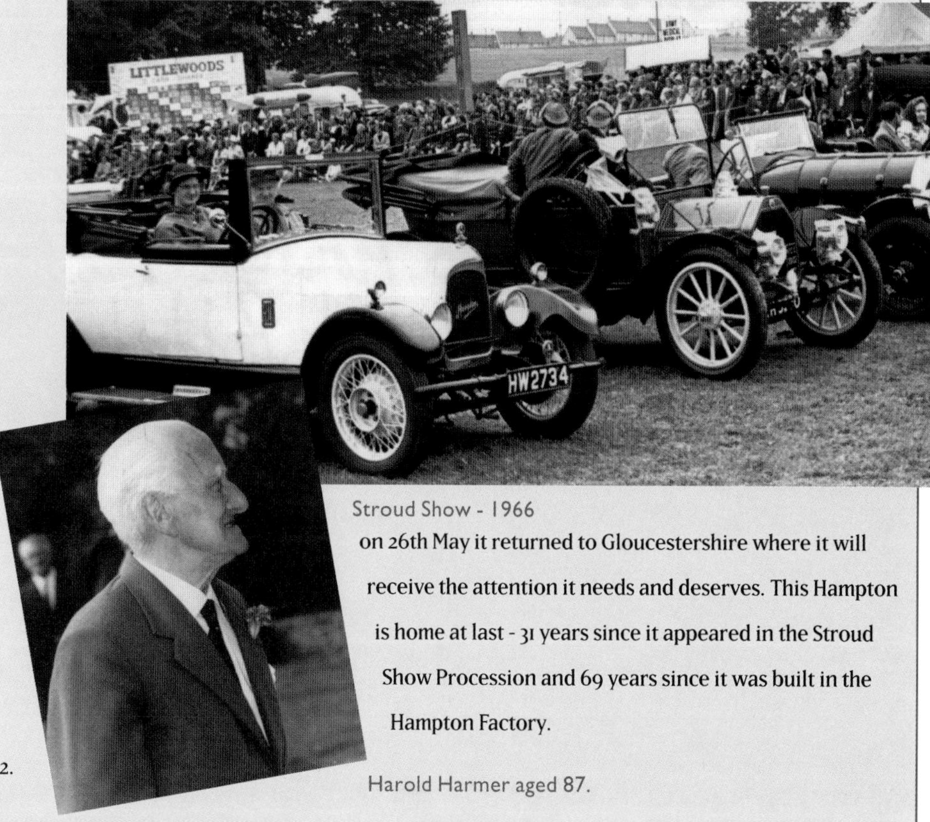

Stroud Show - 1966

Harold Harmer aged 87.

Rosa Cliff Ward became the first owner of a blue Hampton 12hp two seater in April 1930. The car was delivered to her home, Cae Dai in Denbigh. The dealer would almost certainly have been A.H. Meldrum of Denbigh who had been an agent since 1922. The car was used locally by her throughout the Thirties but on the outbreak of war it was sold to William Williams who converted it into a sort of pick-up truck - the log book said "Agric. Goods Lorry". It was used during the war, receiving its regular fuel ration to which it was entitled in its new role as a food producing farm vehicle, perhaps the only Hampton to make a direct contribution to the war effort. However, in 1950, it was abandoned and has not been on the Welsh roads since. It was re-discovered in a very sorry state by a garage owner in Denbigh and around 1980 he sold it for £650 to the present owner, Mr. Sparrow Harrison, who is the nephew of the original owner and now lives at Cae Dai House, thus returning this Hampton to its original home. Apart from being interested in old cars, Mr.Harrison is a keen athlete and amateur boxing coach. He is the founder of the Cae Dai Trust which he established to provide sympathetic surroundings for people in need of support to re-build their lives in a farmhouse style environment.

UN 3456 is one of the last batch of five 4 cylinder 12hp cars to be built and is mechanically similar to **HW 2734**; this confirms that there was very little development taking place on the smaller cars in the 1928/30 period. As shown in the pictures very little of the bodywork has survived but the standard 2 seater and dickey with loose hood and sidescreens would probably have been correct.

The engine is the Meadows 4ED-12/40 (sports) with three main bearings. It is not to be confused with the Brooklands 4ED which had twin carburettors, tulip valves, high lift camshaft with increased valve overlap and a higher compression ratio (7 to 1). This engine has a 26MH Solex carburettor although a Zenith 30HAZ was also an option. Closer examination of the photograph and the Meadows catalogue specifications clearly show that this is the standard engine/clutch/5A gearbox unit as offered by them. The various special cast covers with the Hampton insignia have now all been abandoned as a further cost saving measure. Further Meadows information is included which is also relevant to **HW 2734** in the previous chapter. Some restoration work has taken place on the engine and radiator but more work including a fuel tank and steering wheel will be required before it is ready to receive any bodywork. Unfortunately, its original road wheels were totally beyond repair so it has been necessary to substitute a similar set of the same size but of different configuration. At the time of writing some of this car's documentation has been mislaid which would perhaps have thrown more light on the car's appearance when Sparrow's aunt was the owner. A significant feature of the car is the Hatton-Hall crest on the radiator (pictured above) instead of the Hampton badge, as used on the 1928 cars. It is slightly smaller and less elaborate than the

UN 3456

badge on the Milward Hampton which was originally destined for the larger Empire models.

Whilst Sparrow Harrison spends much of his time directing his Trust, he has also developed an interesting Fifties museum within his farm complex which contains a fascinating display of memorabilia and classic cars which he believes has therapeutic value. His most intriguing vehicle is the original Austin lorry (BPA 260) used by Ronnie Biggs in The Great Train Robbery complete with false bottom to store the loot.

Views of UN 3456 - As found about 1980 with flat bed body.

Although without its bodywork it is important that **UN 3456** has survived because it helps us to understand the very last mechanical development of the 4 cylinder Hampton. Whilst the design and creation of a new body is a formidable task there exists the opportunity of gleaning dimensional information from **HW 2734** which has an identical chassis and bodywork of a similar style. Perhaps in the future, some of Rosa Cliff Ward's original photographs will come to light which would add an extra dimension to this challenging re-construction.

Rosa Cliff Ward OBE

Cae Dai Trust - a family tradition.
Cae Dai has a remarkable history of helping those who are most vulnerable and in need of support. At the end of the War, Rosa Ward, OBE, Principal of the Guide International Service, was involved with re-housing "displaced persons" from concentration camps in Germany and Poland. Cae Dai was used for training people for this work. Following in Rosa Ward's footsteps is her nephew, Sparrow Harrison, who grew up at Cae Dai and founded the Cae Dai Trust in 1992.

Views of UN 3456 chassis.

Gear lever showing gate.

Meadows 12/40 engine/gearbox unit

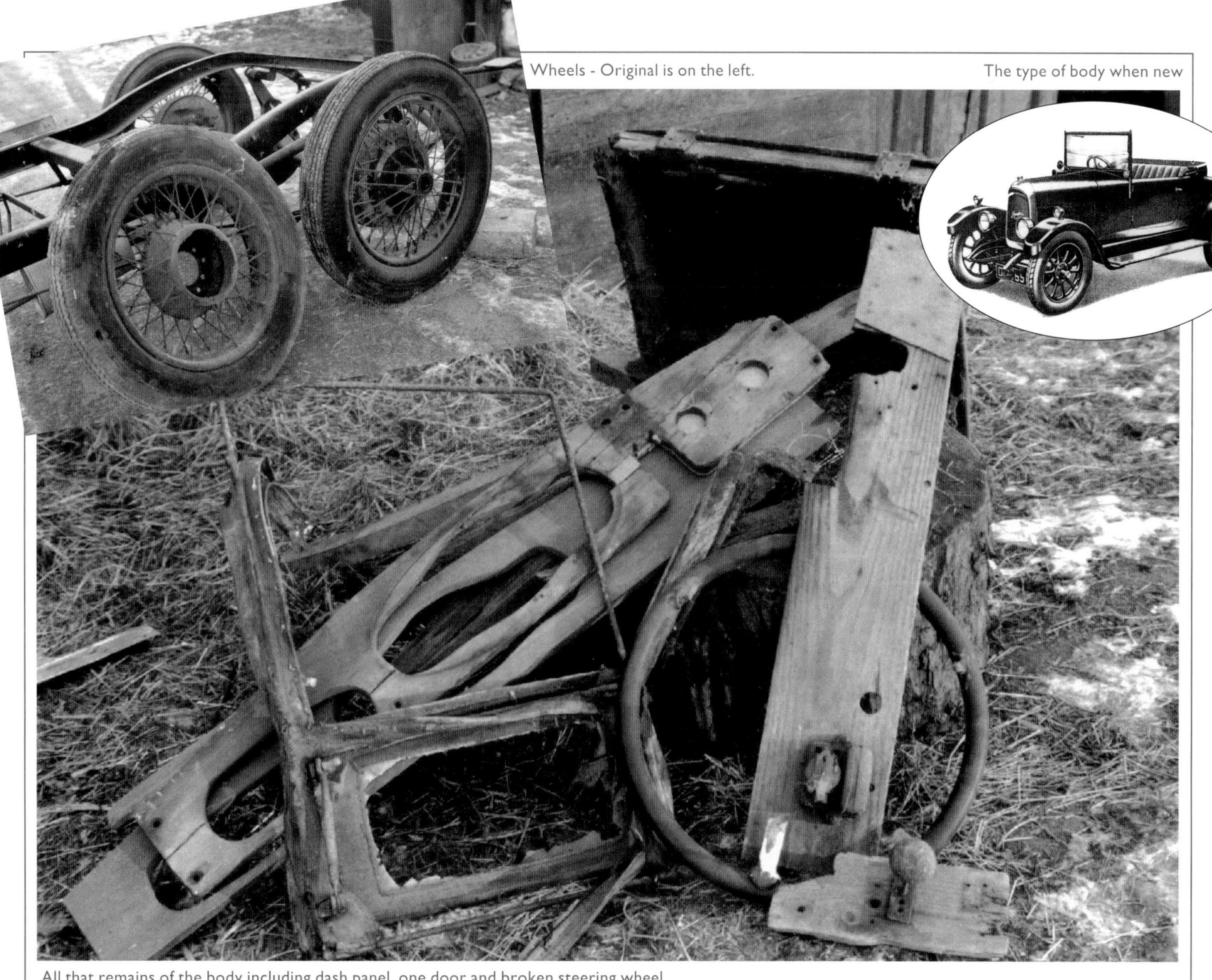
Wheels - Original is on the left.
The type of body when new

All that remains of the body including dash panel, one door and broken steering wheel.

Hampton Cars

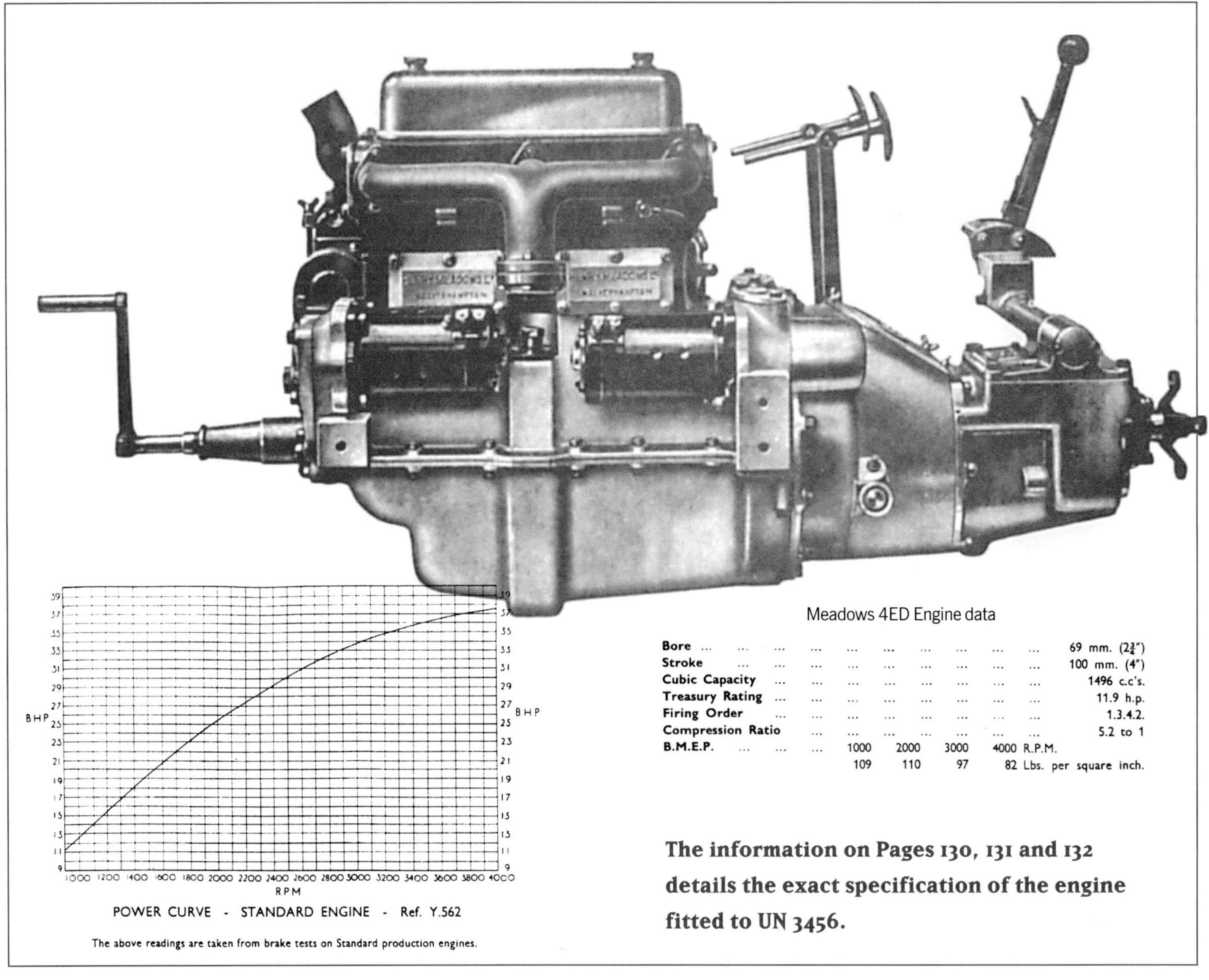

POWER CURVE - STANDARD ENGINE - Ref. Y.562

The above readings are taken from brake tests on Standard production engines.

Meadows 4ED Engine data

Bore					69 mm. ($2\frac{3}{4}$")
Stroke					100 mm. (4")
Cubic Capacity					1496 c.c's.
Treasury Rating					11.9 h.p.
Firing Order					1.3.4.2.
Compression Ratio					5.2 to 1
B.M.E.P.	1000	2000	3000	4000	R.P.M.
	109	110	97	82	Lbs. per square inch.

The information on Pages 130, 131 and 132 details the exact specification of the engine fitted to UN 3456.

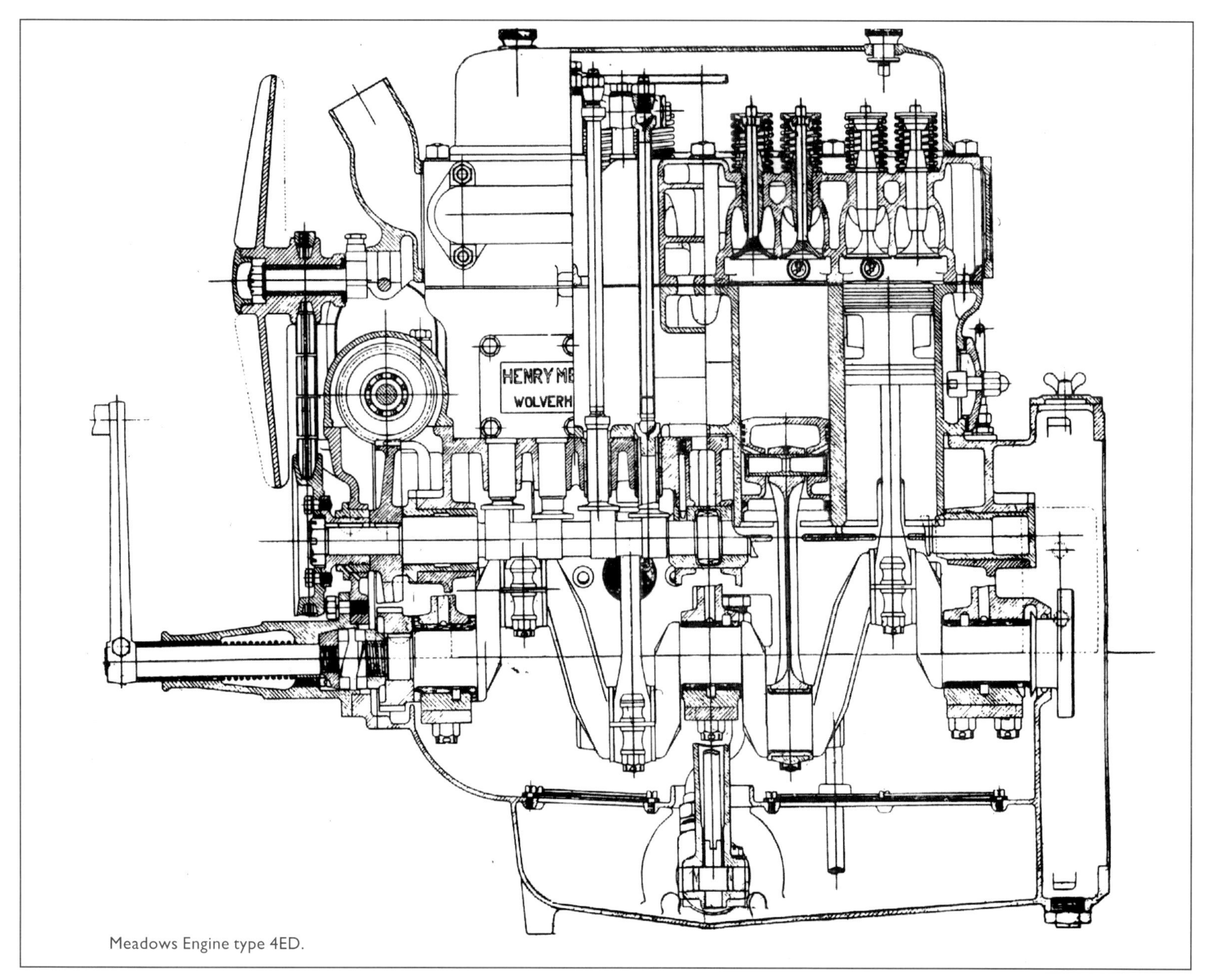

Meadows Engine type 4ED.

Specification Standard Meadows Engine Type 4ED.

Cylinder Block & Head	Monobloc, in special grade, hard grey iron, bored and ground. Water jackets of ample size. Bores tested to 500 lbs. per square inch. Cylinder block detachable from crankcase. Detachable cylinder head with machined combustion chambers.	Valves	Overhead, machined from 3% nickel steel stampings, hardened and ground. Split conical cotters.
Crankcase	Aluminium, divided longitudinally. Crankshaft carried in three die-cast white metal bearings in upper part of crankcase. Flywheel housing cast integral with crankcase, machined to S.A.E standard No. 5. Oil sump capacity 1 gallon.	Lubrication	Fully forced lubrication to crankshaft, camshaft, overhead valve gear, large capacity submerged gear type oil pump, driven from camshaft by vertical shaft and skew gear. Filters on suction and delivery of pump. Adjustable oil pressure relief valve. Dip stick.
Crankshaft	High tensile steel stamping, heat treated, ground and balanced. Diameter 46mm on journals and 45mm on pins.	Ignition	High tension magneto, driven by cross-shaft with ball journal and thrust bearings. Vernier type coupling permitting timing adjustment within 1 degree. Normal timing 45 degrees before T.D.C. fully advanced - may be increased by 10 to 15 degrees for maximum power at 3000 R.P.M. and above.
Connecting Rods	H section steel stampings. White metal big end bearings metalled direct to rods. Caps secured by fitted nickel steel bolts. Small end clamped on 3/4" diameter pin.	Starting Handle	Self contained starting handle asssembly. Starting crank, steel stamping with brass handle.
		Exhaust Manifold	Central discharge type.
Pistons	Die-cast aluminium, fitted with 3 compression rings and 1 scraper ring.	Cooling	Thermo-syphon circulation. Fan available as optional extra.
Camshafts and Tappets	Camshaft formed from solid bar with cams integral, ground and hardened, carried in three bearings, driven by helical gearing. Camshaft wheel of phosphor bronze; driving pinion of steel. Cast iron tappet guides. Tubular push rods with ball and socket joints and accessible adjustment. Valve rockers, steel stampings, hardened on contact face, fitted with gunmetal bushes, carried on hollow steel shafts mounted in bronze brackets.	Dynamo	Provision for mounting on near side, drive by silent helical gear, completely enclosed, running in oil.
		Flywheel	Flywheel, steel stamping, machined all over, carefully balanced, spigoted on crankshaft, secured by four bolts. Teeth cut on rim for starter engagement.
		Clutch	Twin plate cork lined, running in oil.

The Milward Hampton is the very last survivor of the group and over the years has attracted much publicity because it is a unique vehicle. Its history is well documented and as it is now complete and running will continue to attract attention. Its owner is Dennis Beedle of Bristol who has patiently restored it over the past 36 years. Blenheim House at Randwick (some two miles north of Dudbridge) was the home of Mr. and Mrs. William Milward whilst he was the General Manager and for a period a director of Hampton Cars. When he resigned in mid 1931 he took with him enough Hampton parts to build a car for his own use. Whether he actually bid for these parts at the final Auction Sale or negotiated to buy them independently is not clear but it is known that there was considerable animosity between Thomas Godman, the Receiver, and Milward regarding the terms under which the latter would finally leave the Company after eight years of high level and dedicated service. Much of the unpleasantness, no doubt, centred around the Röhr 8 cylinder engine imported from Germany which had been removed from the large Show car saloon known as **GN 5599**. A general view of this engine and gearbox is shown in Chapter 9. Some sort of legal battle is suggested but as both men were financially stretched at that time litigation is unlikely. However, local sources were of the opinion that the "loss" of the engine was reported to the police who for reasons best known to themselves did not pursue the matter.

DG 5009

Perhaps they were satisfied with Milward's explanation of his acquisition or was it Godman's political affiliation that switched them off ? Nonetheless, Milward had left with most of the parts required to construct a car, including the jewel in the crown, the straight eight engine, and quickly set about designing and building his own Hampton in the Coach House at his home. He sought the assistance of Edgar Fowles, one of his former body builders from the factory. In his own words Edgar said "Regarding the last Hampton ever made, I plead guilty to building the body. I built it while on the dole, not expecting to be paid for it." He went on to say "the sporting type was put together in a kind of coach house at Blenheim House". Later, Mrs. Milward told Max that some parts were also put together in the kitchen - it seems that car enthusiasts have been doing this sort of thing for many years - the author included. Cleaning the cylinder head prior to assembly was, however, carried out in the garden with the help of the family dog. The resulting vehicle with its smart aluminium body took about one year to construct and was first registered on 5th August 1932.

The four seater, **DG 5009**, was never intended to have independent suspension and judging by the weight and bulk of this chassis, parts of a 3 litre chassis were used. For example the rear chassis cross member is made from a channel section of 1/4" thickness. It has a track of 48" which is the same as the smaller 4

cylinder Hampton car but the wheel base is some 2" shorter at 109". The rear suspension is a low slung semi-elliptic design, with the front end based on the 12hp cars' standard suspension. The radiator surround is very similar to the Empire Six and careful examination reveals that this was achieved by brazing an extended section on to the bottom of a normal shell. The Hatton-Hall crest suggests that this had previously been used on another car. The tall radiator gives the whole car a rather high bonnet line. There is no evidence to suggest that this vehicle was a prototype sports car that Hamptons were considering producing. It was simply a low cost venture to provide Mr. & Mrs. Milward with daily transport, using a most interesting engine which was available at the time. They retained the car until William's death in 1946. During the war he was general manager of The Coventry Victor Motor Company of Coventry in charge of war time production, then living in Kenilworth.

After the war Mrs. Margaret Milward lived at "Daneway", Bowbridge Lane, Stroud and in 1947 sold **DG 5009** to Mr. F.L. Adams who lived in Churchdown, Gloucester at that time. Adams fitted a four speed Rover gearbox in place of the Aphon original and also added an outside exhaust system. He completely overhauled the eight cylinder Röhr engine, fitted conventional cycle type front wings and finally painted the whole car red.

In 1953 he needed a family saloon so the Hampton was sold to Peter Rawling

William Milward - Hands-on engineering at Blenheim House.

Mr. & Mrs. Milward enjoying their Hampton on the Brecon Beacons.

from Cranham who ran it for a year or so before passing it on to Derek Wasley in Gloucester. Its first move out of Gloucestershire was in 1955 to William Hirst of Crudwell who taxed it for 3 months then consigned it to the rear of his scrap yard. Thankfully, it was re-discovered in 1961, but in a very dilapidated condition, by Dennis Beedle who purchased it for £25 late one evening just before two other prospective purchasers emerged from the shadows.

The car was originally built with a round scuttle mounted fuel tank but by the

Mr. & Mrs. F.L. Adams at Vinegar Hill Farm, Oxlynch.

Crankshaft/piston assembly Röhr 8 cylinder engine. Note:- nine main bearings and counterbalanced design.

time Dennis became involved this had been moved to the rear of the car and secured with pieces of wire. An SU 6 volt electric fuel pump had also been added. However, the tank is now installed correctly under the scuttle but a fuel pump has been retained. The 11.5 gallon tank, almost certainly from a 3 litre saloon, has received several modifications over the years but there is evidence that Milward built the car to operate with gravity feed and also incorporated a Hobson telegauge which had been the practice on earlier Hamptons. The body is now painted Hampton Grey. The Milward Hampton paid a nostalgic visit to its birthplace, Blenheim House and also Rodborough Fort in March 1997. Despite poor weather the resulting photographs can be seen on Pages 137 and in the colour section.

Röhr 8. Plug shroud & connector

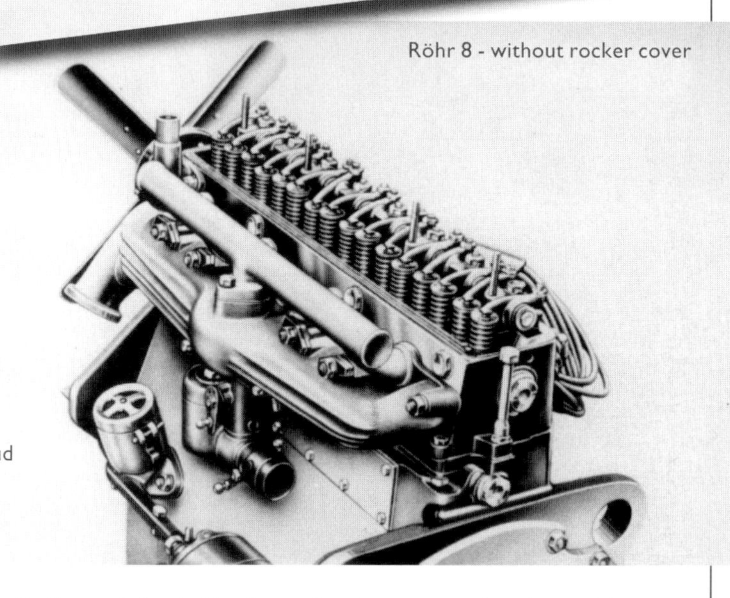

Röhr 8 - without rocker cover

1961. Dennis examines his new Hampton.

Röhr Engine Specification

8 cylinders in line, overhead valves, push rod operated.
60mm bore x 100mm stroke. Capacity 2.262 cc.
Compression ratio 5.8 to 1. Output 50hp.
6 volt electrics, Bosch distributor, coil,
starter & dynamo.
18mm Bosch plugs, No. M95-TI 80+ short reach.
Solex Carburettor type K-30 MOV.
Water pump & fan assisted cooling.

Röhr Straight Eight engine.

Fuel tank re-located under the scuttle.

Dennis & Mary Beedle.

Rodborough Fort in the mist 1997.

9
The beginning of the end - From Fantasy to Fascism

1929 R Type Röhr Roadster

On his appointment in July 1930, Thomas Godman swiftly brought to a halt the meagre production at the Dudbridge factory and most of the remaining workers were laid off. His was undoubtedly the toughest job of the procession of Receivers that Hampton Cars had had to endure and he was probably the most inexperienced to tackle the task - for this was not an assignment for an opportunist.

The last two 10 hp Meadows engines had arrived in May, had been installed in cars and sold. So Godman was not faced with cars to sell - in fact he was the only Receiver who was not obliged to carry on active trading for very long. He made no serious attempt to sell the business as a going concern which is hardly surprising as he had no order book, a loss making history and a serious credibility problem. However, he had a responsibility for tying up the affairs of Hampton Cars (London) Ltd. and returning some capital to John Hatton-Hall so in addition to William Milward he retained a small staff who spent part of their time on this work and the rest on his new project. Later in 1930, not long after the factory ceased production, Thomas Godman was seriously investigating the possibility of producing a much more advanced Hampton car, based loosely on the lines of the 3 litre Empire Saloon. Was this a recurrence of the strange phenomenon of "falling in love with Hampton Cars" or did he accept the Receivership with something up his sleeve ? - the latter is suspected.

Godman had a German wife and had many high level contacts in her country. Although he described himself as a designer and financial adviser, his early training was as a merchant seaman and in the 1914/18 war, a submarine navigating officer. His mother-in-law, Mrs. Annie Kohler, who lived with them, reputedly financed the purchase of their home - the elegant Cainscross House - with funds from a family business in Germany, manufacturing

CAINSCROSS HOUSE
An exceptionally well-built Residence containing 4 Reception Rooms, Billiard Room, 9 Bed and Dressing Rooms, Bath Room, etc., facing south, lighted by electric light, and having public water supply and drainage, and standing in attractive Grounds, with excellent Modern STABLING, GLASS HOUSES, KITCHEN GARDENS, COTTAGE and ENCLOSURES OF PASTURE LAND, the whole comprising about 13.5 Acres.

Geneva Motor Show 1929.

ammunition. Godman was about 50 years old and had spent 20 years in Germany and some time in America. With his background it is not too surprising that he was soon in touch with Hans Gustav Röhr, a talented engineer, who had made a reputation for himself in the German aviation industry during the 1914/18 War. During the Twenties he turned his attention to the production of advanced suspension systems for automobiles. Werner Schollenberger has recently compiled an extensive history of Röhr and his career which has helped the author to clarify some interesting links with the Hampton story.

Whilst only being able to highlight a few significant details of the Röhr involvement, there is little doubt that Godman must have been aware of the developments taking place in car suspension systems in Germany. Röhr's factory in Ober-Ramstadt, near Frankfurt, had previously been used for the manufacture of ammunition (remember mother-in-law) and after the war Adler and Senator typewriters were made there. The Falcon car was produced in the works between 1921 and 1925. In 1926 Röhr Autowerke A.G. was established to produce Röhr's own cars and those

Berlin Motor Show 1928.

DER RÖHR
INTERNATIONALE
AUTOMOBIL-AUSSTELLUNG
BERLIN 1928:
HALLE I, STAND 57
TELEF. WESTEND 6618
IT-15245
8 Cylinder
ist der Zeit vorausgeeilt
R
BEACHTEN SIE SEINE UNERREICHTEN
FAHREIGENSCHAFTEN, BEDINGT DURCH:
DIE SCHWINGHINTERACHSE
ACHSLOSE VORDERRAD-AUFHÄNGUNG
NEUARTIGEN TIEFBAURAHMEN
GROSSTES ANZUGSVERMOGEN
UND HOCHSTE ELASTIZITAT DES MOTORS
REIN DEUTSCHES FABRIKAT DER
PREIS:
4–5 SITZIGES CABRIOLET
RM 8250.-
RÖHR-AUTO AG
OBER-RAMSTADT (HESSEN)

Röhr Automobile Factory at Ober-Ramstadt.

Röhr 4 Door Saloon - 1928.

illustrated come from 1928/30. In the early autumn of 1930, a Röhr (8-R) fully independent chassis complete with eight cylinder engine and gearbox arrived at Dudbridge. This chassis would have contained the features shown in the cut away drawing overleaf; double transverse leaf springs at the front with cantilever springs at the rear. The essence of the independently sprung rear axle is that the central final drive unit is

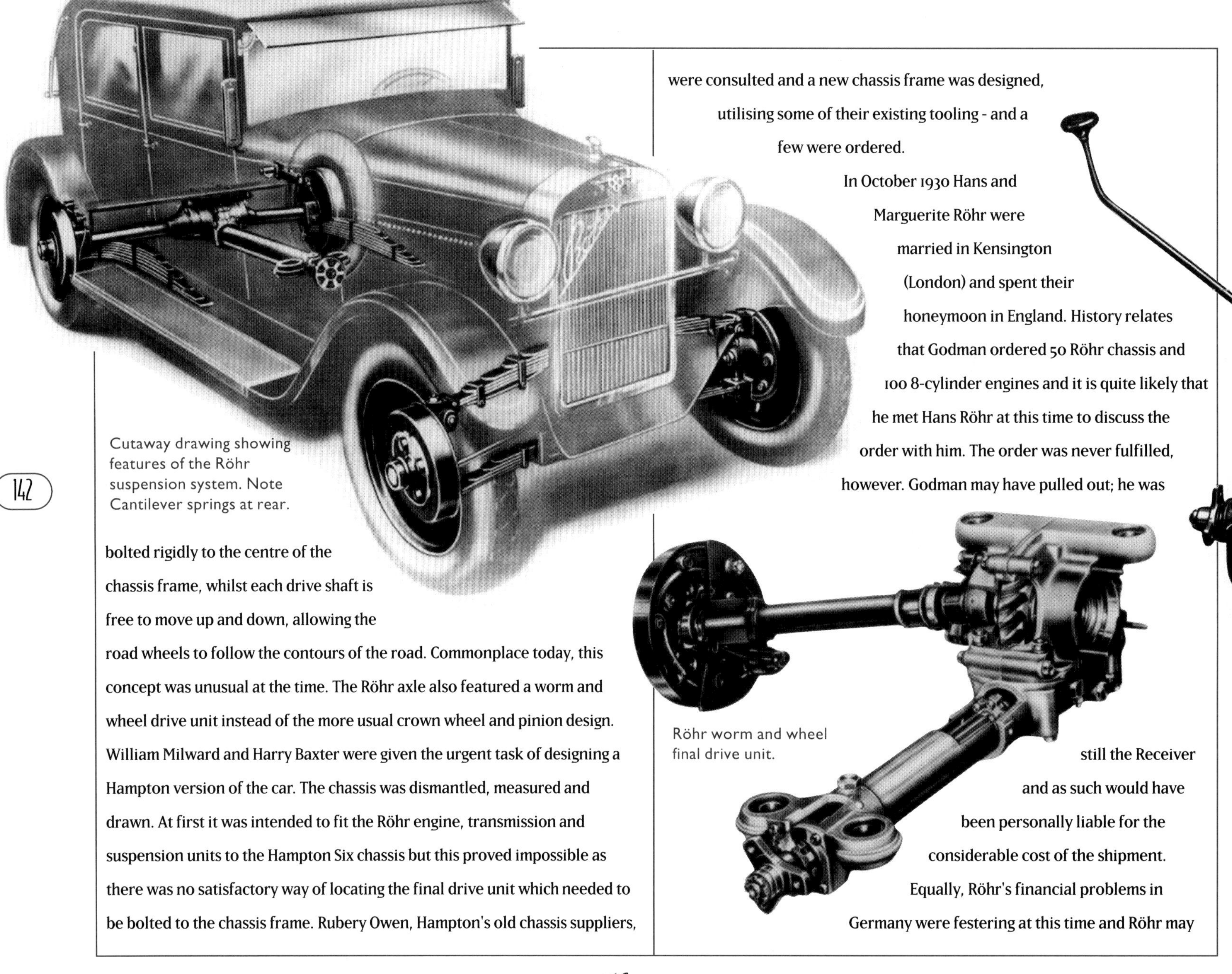

Cutaway drawing showing features of the Röhr suspension system. Note Cantilever springs at rear.

Röhr worm and wheel final drive unit.

bolted rigidly to the centre of the chassis frame, whilst each drive shaft is free to move up and down, allowing the road wheels to follow the contours of the road. Commonplace today, this concept was unusual at the time. The Röhr axle also featured a worm and wheel drive unit instead of the more usual crown wheel and pinion design. William Milward and Harry Baxter were given the urgent task of designing a Hampton version of the car. The chassis was dismantled, measured and drawn. At first it was intended to fit the Röhr engine, transmission and suspension units to the Hampton Six chassis but this proved impossible as there was no satisfactory way of locating the final drive unit which needed to be bolted to the chassis frame. Rubery Owen, Hampton's old chassis suppliers, were consulted and a new chassis frame was designed, utilising some of their existing tooling - and a few were ordered.

In October 1930 Hans and Marguerite Röhr were married in Kensington (London) and spent their honeymoon in England. History relates that Godman ordered 50 Röhr chassis and 100 8-cylinder engines and it is quite likely that he met Hans Röhr at this time to discuss the order with him. The order was never fulfilled, however. Godman may have pulled out; he was still the Receiver and as such would have been personally liable for the considerable cost of the shipment. Equally, Röhr's financial problems in Germany were festering at this time and Röhr may have had second thoughts about this whole venture and his company's ability to execute the order.

Godman's marketing and engineering development strategy over the next couple of years shows a confused picture indeed - a series of mainly

The 2.262 c.c. 8 Cylinder Röhr engine with 3 speed Warner-Aphon gearbox.

haphazard attempts to salvage some commercial advantage from the remnants of the Hampton business.

Most surprisingly, a Press report in November 1930 announced that Hampton was planning to fit the Cowburn gearbox made by Kitsons Components Ltd. of Stroud to Hampton cars. On 30th January 1931 Kitsons bought part of the

AT LOW RESERVES.

DUDBRIDGE, near STROUD.

Particulars of Sale
of the
Valuable Freehold Modern
FACTORY PREMISES,
forming part of the

HAMPTON CAR WORKS

and comprising :—
Small Compact Factory,
Foundry, Stores, and
Large Yard,
which

Davis, Champion & Payne

will Sell by Auction,
At "The Subscription Rooms," Stroud,
On FRIDAY, MARCH 13th, 1931,
punctually at **6 o'clock,**

Copies of these particulars may be obtained of the AUCTIONEERS, 16, Kendrick Street, Stroud; of T. GODMAN, Esq., 40, Woburn Place, London, W.C.1.; or of Messrs. HEELAS & SHEPPARD, Solicitors, Rowcroft, Stroud.

"Stroud News"

Dudbridge factory from Hamptons, presumably to manufacture their epicyclical gear box which did away with conventional gears and relied upon hardened rollers to transmit the power. As Hamptons were not making any production vehicles at that time this announcement seemed somewhat premature.

The factory was eventually sold at an auction conducted by Davies, Champion & Payne on 13th March 1931 at the Subscription Rooms - the very place which had hosted that Hampton inspirational company dinner way back in 1919. Hamptons were now homeless. However, on the very day that the factory came under the auctioneer's hammer, The Autocar announced Godman's revolutionary new product: namely, a fully independent Sportsman's de-luxe saloon car with the German straight eight (Röhr) engine of 2500cc and the toothless Cowburn gearbox - all for £575. The old 3 litre 6 cylinder de luxe Empire saloon with standard suspension and

Röhr-8 installed in Saloon.

Bekanntmachung.

Das in der Gemarkung Ober-Ramstadt gelegene, gesamte Fabrikanwesen der „Firma Röhr-Auto Akt. Ges." zu Ober-Ramstadt nebst 124825 qm. Ackergrundstücken soll

Freitag, den 26. Juni 1931 nachm. 4 Uhr

vor dem unterzeichneten Gericht im neuen Gerichtsgebäude zu Darmstadt, Mathildenplatz, Saal 118 zwangsweise versteigert werden.

Darmstadt, den 29. April 1931.

Hessisches Amtsgericht II.

Translation
Announcement: The whole of the factory site belonging to Messrs. Röhr Auto Akt.Ges. in Ober-Ramstadt in the district of Ober-Ramstadt together with 124,825 sq. metres of arable land has to be auctioned by Court Order on Friday, 26th June 1931 at 4 pm in the presence of the undersigned magistrate in the new Court Building in Darmstadt, Mathildenplatz, Room 118.
Darmstadt, 29th April 1931. Hesse Magistrate's Court II.

transmission was now a mere £450.

Just four days later The Motor reported more correctly that "the engine size was 2,262cc and that a Warner gearbox (which would have come from the Röhr chassis) was fitted to the only car that has yet been built but that a friction box of new design will be used eventually". Godman was now using Hampton Cars (London) Ltd. at 40 Woburn Place, London as his contact address. This new car was the one on which Baxter and Milward had been burning the midnight oil throughout the winter months.

This prototype, (GN 5599), built in the factory before it was sold, used the Rubery Owen chassis plus independent suspension components of similar design to Röhr's, the 8 cylinder engine and a Warner-Aphon 3 speed gearbox. In addition to the monumental task of assembling these parts, Harry Baxter also had a hand in re-designing the body which was produced by H.H. Martyn of Cheltenham, based on sketches of the Wolverhampton made Star car which he drew at the Olympia Motor Show. Milward, who also contributed significantly to this work, made a press statement in Golfing in March 1931, expressing his belief in the new car and its future. However, the Röhr Company failed in April (instantly cutting off any prospect of engine supplies) and hearing of this Milward must have been both embarrassed and humiliated. This final blow to his credibility hastened his decision to throw in the towel not long afterwards. At that time he negotiated to acquire a kit of car parts, including the Röhr engine which had by now been removed from the prototype. As outlined in the previous Chapter, these parts became the Milward Hampton. His departure was described by many as acrimonious; he certainly did not approve of Godman's methods or style, despite tolerating them for a year.

Godman's input into the new saloon car is difficult to quantify but by any standards it seems incredible that a company now in liquidation with no factory, no significant capital, no support from Germany and a work force of himself, Harry Baxter, Peggy Lodge (Secretary) and a part time gardener, could realistically cope with the development and production of this advanced new motor car - pure fantasy indeed!

The disposal of the factory, however, created yet another problem for Godman as he had no premises in which to continue development work on his new car. The statutory Receiver's records would have been most enlightening had they not been destroyed, because from information gleaned from other

sources, his Receivership style was unusual. Thomas Godman acquired the stock of Hampton cars spares himself and removed them to his residence which had useful stables and outhouses. One must assume the price paid was reasonable and acceptable to the unsecured creditors !

However, during the autumn of 1931, Hampton Cars continued to use Godman's London address in Woburn Place until he conceived the idea of creating The Safety Suspension Car Company at his home, Cainscross House, but still retaining the name Hampton Cars on his letter heading. This was not a limited company - just a sole trading operation with Godman the proprietor. The straight eight engine idea had also now been dropped because of Röhr's company collapse and Godman's lack of technical know-how. His last advertisements only featured a 6 cylinder car with 16hp side valve engine of 2414cc (by USA manufacturer Continental) and made no mention of the Cowburn box. Godman's large two colour four page brochure was the final attempt to gain some customers for the Empire Sportsman part of the text of which is allowed to speak for itself on Page 150. **GN 5599** was a star for a brief period appearing as it did in most sections of the motoring press. How the author wishes it had survived so that the whole world would have been able to evaluate its suspension system in detail.

On October 21st 1931 Thomas Godman registered three Patents in his name (Nos. 392:597/392:598/392:599) detailing his suspension system. These may have been prepared several months previously in conjunction with Hans Röhr, but comparison with some of the Röhr patents shows several variances. In the case of the front suspension, Godman seems to have followed Röhr's design closely as we see by comparing his patent 392.598 with Röhr's Patent 485.932 (prepared two years earlier) - and with the cutaway drawing of the Röhr car on Page 142.

Godman's rear axle, however, illustrated in his Patent 392.597, whilst designed to be bolted directly to the chassis like Röhr's, has reverted to a

The Hampton Sportsman saloon.

Röhr rear axle layout. An identical picture appeared in Autocar 30.10.31 - as a Hampton product.

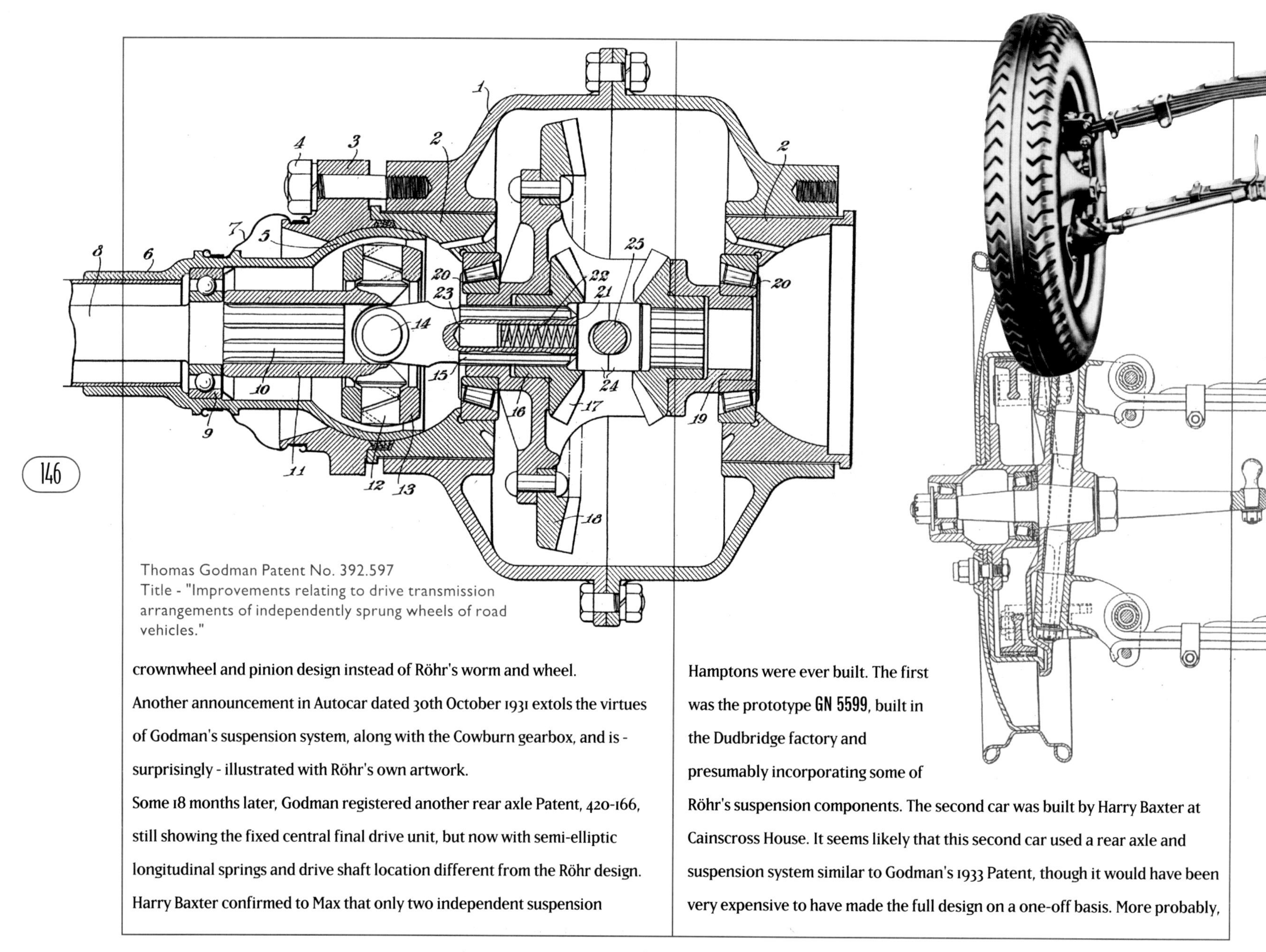

Thomas Godman Patent No. 392.597
Title - "Improvements relating to drive transmission arrangements of independently sprung wheels of road vehicles."

crownwheel and pinion design instead of Röhr's worm and wheel.

Another announcement in Autocar dated 30th October 1931 extols the virtues of Godman's suspension system, along with the Cowburn gearbox, and is - surprisingly - illustrated with Röhr's own artwork.

Some 18 months later, Godman registered another rear axle Patent, 420-166, still showing the fixed central final drive unit, but now with semi-elliptic longitudinal springs and drive shaft location different from the Röhr design. Harry Baxter confirmed to Max that only two independent suspension Hamptons were ever built. The first was the prototype **GN 5599**, built in the Dudbridge factory and presumably incorporating some of Röhr's suspension components. The second car was built by Harry Baxter at Cainscross House. It seems likely that this second car used a rear axle and suspension system similar to Godman's 1933 Patent, though it would have been very expensive to have made the full design on a one-off basis. More probably,

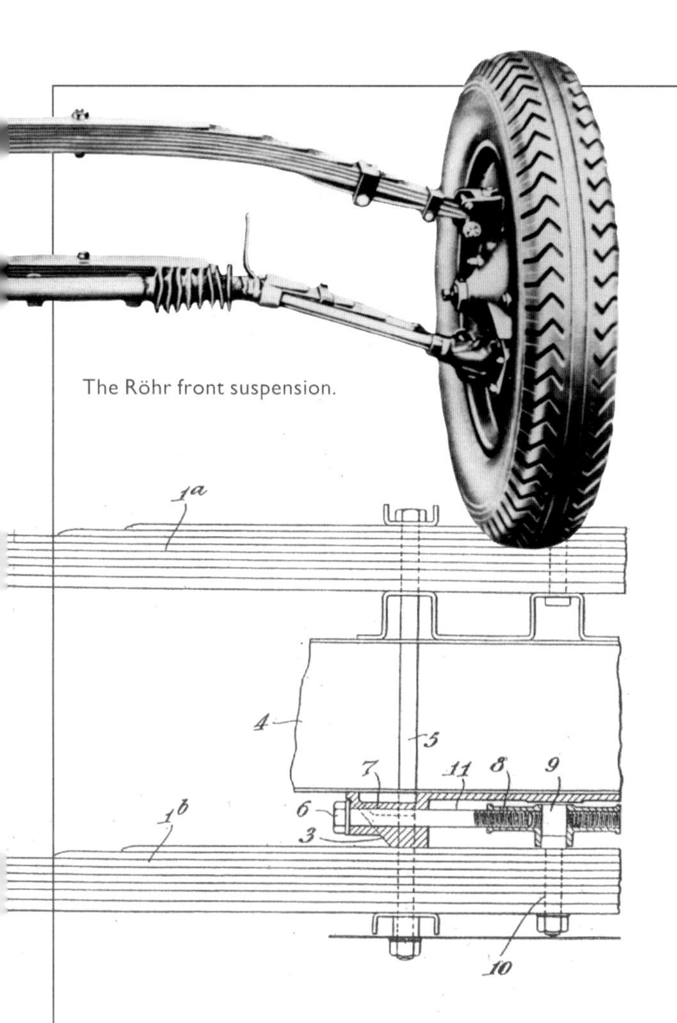

The Röhr front suspension.

Thomas Godman Patent No. 392.598
Title - "Improvements in transverse suspension arrangements for road vehicles".

DEUTSCHES REICH

AUSGEGEBEN AM
8. NOVEMBER 1929

REICHSPATENTAMT

PATENTSCHRIFT

№ 485 932

KLASSE **63c** GRUPPE 38/03

R 77948 II/63c

Tag der Bekanntmachung über die Erteilung des Patents: 24. Oktober 1929

Gustav Röhr in Oberramstadt, Hessen

Vorrichtung zum Einstellen des Sturzes der Vorderräder von Kraftfahrzeugen

Abb. 1

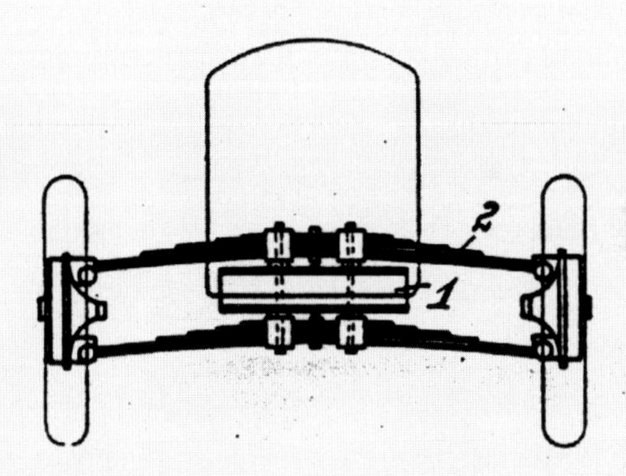

Röhr front suspension layout. Several of his patents covered the linking and securing of this unit to the chassis frame e.g. Röhr patent 485.932 shows very similar features but not identical with Godman's.

we speculate that they would have cut down a conventional solid back axle and fitted flanges and fabric couplings outboard of the crown wheel and pinion assembly.

We know that a black car with red upholstery, fully independent rear suspension and Continental side valve engine was later sold to Mr. Ron Taylor of Gloucester around 1936. He subsequently replaced the rear suspension first with a Morris, then with an Essex solid back axle because "the fabric joints could not stand the constant flexing". Its last known resting place was Tickles Garage of Burnham on Sea. This was almost certainly the Cainscross House built Hampton as the original Röhr system did not have any fabric joints. The fate of **GN 5599** remains a mystery.

Sadly, Max did not question Harry Baxter intensively on these details so the world will never know for certain which components made up the rear suspension and drive train of either of the Empire Sportsman cars.

Godman had high hopes for his Suspension System and stated on his letter heading "Pioneers and Patentees of British Independently sprung Chassis for all Road Transport" - a bold claim indeed. Clearly, the concept was German but his version could reasonably be described as British. To his credit, he worked hard to sell the system to other manufacturers when he realised that developing the idea himself was way beyond his financial and technical resources. Harry Baxter certainly fitted a form of this suspension to a Riley Nine chassis and personally delivered it to Coventry for Victor Riley himself to evaluate. He was apparently very pleased with the handling and road holding but no orders were placed. A similar conversion was carried out on a Triumph Gloria chassis but also with a negative response; perhaps it was ahead of its time or just too expensive for the tough

Thomas Godman's later Patent No. 420.166 27th May 1933
Title - "Improvements in the suspension of road vehicles provided with independently sprung wheels".

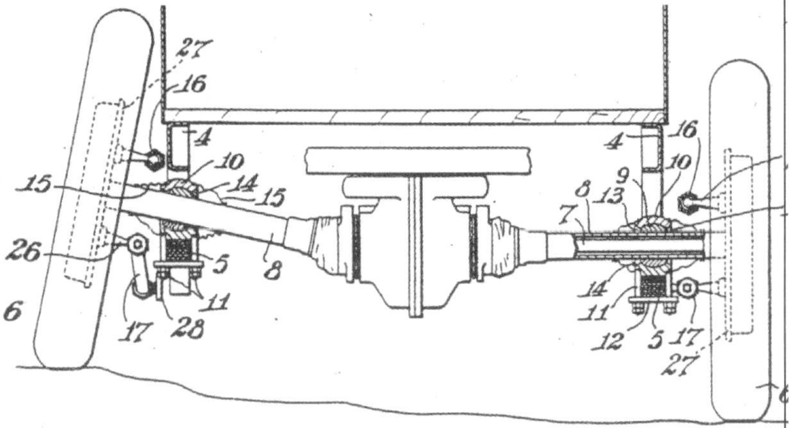

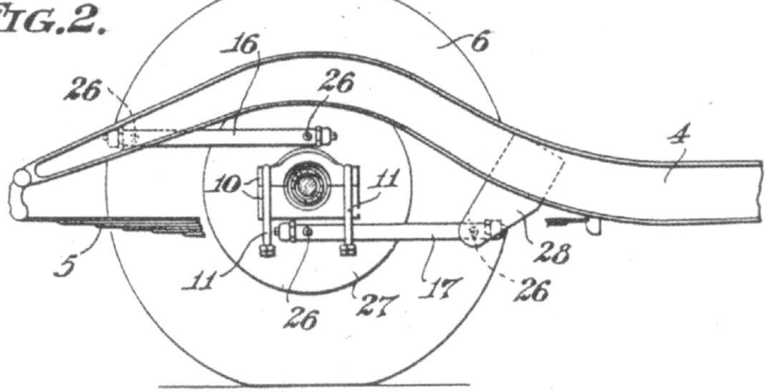

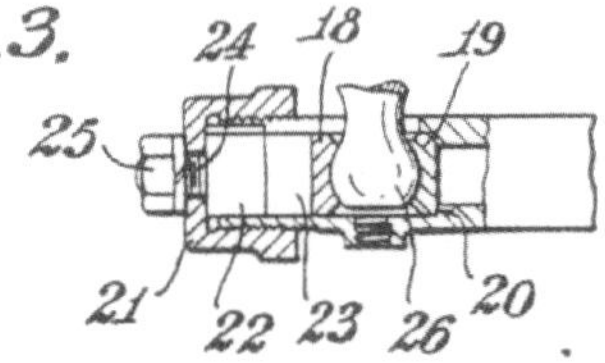

GN5599. Not used in the publicity shots - Frank Pick, a long serving employee.

conditions in the early 1930's when cart springs and solid axles were the order of the day on family motorcars. Baxter told Max that the system worked well and was unequalled in his experience, though of course this had all been gained at Hamptons where he had started as a boy.

Whilst Harry Baxter is known to have produced drawings of the Röhr system suspension components, he said he had no knowledge of Godman or Röhr's patents which were unfortunately not available when Max discussed the subject with him in 1969. Only the present research has unearthed them. Perhaps, Thomas Godman employed another draughtsman to produce the information to accompany his patent applications or, more likely, chose to claim Harry's work for himself, being more worldly in these matters. Harry left

Godman's employ in 1933 along with Peggy Lodge (later Mrs. Ollerenshaw). One of the last letters that Peggy typed was to Mr. C.W. Moss of Sheffield (a disgruntled customer) which confirmed Godman's policy at that time, although he was obviously still prepared to trade in spares of the earlier Hampton models if he had stock - useful pocket money no doubt. Harry spent a couple of years with Whitfield Engineering (on the old Hampton factory site) before taking an appointment with the Gloucester

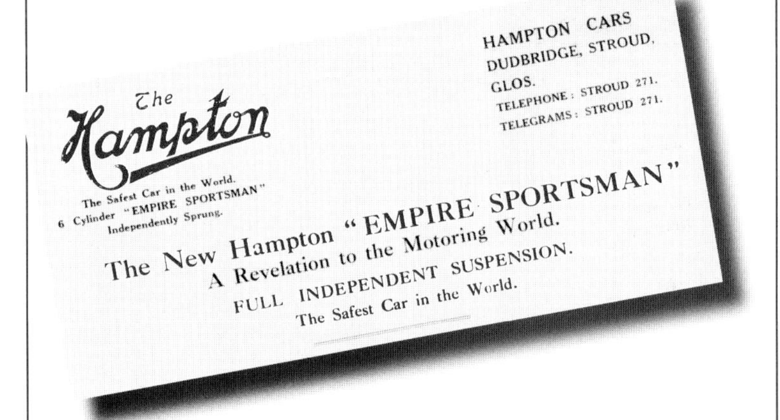

Brief Specification

Engine		Central chassis lubrication	
Six cylinder with side valves		Disc wheels with	
67mm bore x 114mm stroke		Dunlop tyres 30 inches x 5.5 inches	
Capacity 2414cc. RAC rating 16.7hp		Leather upholstery	
Stromberg or Zenith carburettor			
Fuel supply : 12v electric pump		Wheelbase	10 foot 9inches
Tank at rear - 14 gallons		Track	4 foot 8inches
Gearbox		Length overall	14 foot 3 inches
4 speed		Width overall	5 foot 8 inches
Ratios : 4.8, 7.4, 11.3, 18.06		Height overall	5foot 2 inches
Brakes :		Ground clearance	9.5 inches
With vacuum servo		Weight unladen	23 cwt.

Thomas Godman as copy-writer!

Behold! A new era has opened up for all motorists with the advent of the New Hampton "EMPIRE SPORTSMAN".

Pioneers of progressive car construction, first in the field with advanced ideas, bearing in mind always that the paramount necessities of the motorist in this age of progress are safety and speed, we present to the motorist our Independently sprung model, proved by us to be the "safest car in the World." After years of painstaking experiments under all road conditions, both at Home and Abroad, we have produced a chassis embodying a suspension system which gives the motorist the maximum of safety. In addition, the New Hampton "EMPIRE SPORTSMAN" is a car that immediately catches the eye with the beauty of its design and is as much a pleasure to ride in as it is to behold.

Everyone has, of course, heard of the "Seven Wonders of the World" but the producers of the New Hampton may well lay claim to having created the Eighth.

Roads, rough or smooth, are all alike to this wonderful car which, owing to its unique method of independent suspension, is impervious to all obstacles which would spell disaster to the ordinary car. Pot-holes, curbs, deep gutters, level crossings and all such pitfalls are ignored and unnoticed.

The most vital point in which this cars excels, however, beyond all others is the absence of skidding. Corners can be negotiated at high speed without the fear of this great danger, the danger that has been the cause of so much loss of life. No matter how wet or greasy the road, this car will neither roll nor skid and so eliminates entirely the strain at present imposed on the driver and enables him to maintain an average road speed hitherto unheard of.

Our 16hp "EMPIRE SPORTSMAN", particulars of which are given here, is the last word in chassis construction, suitable for use under any road conditions in any part of the World.

The wheels, with their independent movement, localize and deal with all shocks and the driving comfort of this car is infinitely superior to anything on the road.

Priced £525, we give a car of polished elegance, incredible safety and power.

Too little attention has been given in the past to chassis improvements and, as a matter of fact, chassis in general today do not differ in construction from those of 25 years ago.

It has been left to the Hampton engineers to deal with this vital question of progressive chassis construction and in this model we give to the public, without fear, a car which challenges the World of Motoring in that we claim it to be the "Safest car in the World." The new Hampton "EMPIRE SPORTSMAN" will revolutionize the World of Motoring and all discerning motorists will insist on having this great boon to safety which has been so long delayed and which is backed by the best British brains and workmanship.

Our car has the lowest centre of gravity known and cannot possibly overturn.

ALL LETTERS TO BE ADDRESSED TO THE FIRM AND NOT TO INDIVIDUALS

CODES:
A.B.C. 6TH EDITION

Hampton Cars

PROPRIETORS

THE SAFETY SUSPENSION CAR COMPANY

(THOMAS GODMAN)

CAINSCROSS, STROUD, GLOS.

TELEPHONE NO. 271 STROUD.
TELEGRAMS 271 STROUD.

OUR REF. TG/PL
YOUR REF.

PIONEERS AND PATENTEES OF BRITISH INDEPENDENTLY SPRUNG CHASSIS FOR ALL ROAD TRANSPORT

15th February, 1933.

C.W. Moss Esq.,
16, Devonshire Road,
Totley Rise,
Nr. Sheffield.

Dear Sir,

Replying to your gently reproving letter of the 13th inst.

My interest is, of course, compelled by such a letter, but, in explanation of my apparent neglect I would state that I have not interested in previous Hampton Cars beyond the supplying of Spares.

The name was taken over by me in order to give a name to my new Independently Sprung Car of which I am the Patentee and Designer and particulars of same are enclosed herewith.

I also enclose an outline drawing of the old Hampton Gearbox, but, if you require spares all you have to do is to let me know what you want and if possible send the part or the number.

I most cordially agree that we appear to be wasteing each others time.

Yours truly,
FOR THE SAFETY SUSPENSION CAR CO.

Thomas Godman

THOMAS GODMAN
Proprietor

Encls:

Mrs Peggy Ollerenshaw now residing in Dorchester.

Aircraft Company at Hucclecote. Initially, he was involved with the Gladiator and later became chief liaison officer on the Typhoon project. His thirteen years employment with Hampton Cars covered almost the total life of the Dudbridge operation; he was their longest serving employee. Despite the many ups and downs he claimed that these were "some of the best years of his career".

During 1933 Thomas Godman was reluctantly trading in his dwindling stock of spares for the older models but in reality the Hampton Story was finally over - the prototype building of the past couple of years had somehow come back full circle to the early days in 1911 when William Paddon was experimenting with various automobile designs in Birmingham. Perhaps beginning to tire of his venture into the motor industry, Godman became an active member of Sir Oswald Mosley's British Union of Fascists who had a Stroud branch called the Empire Club in John Street. In 1934, Sir Oswald Mosley came to Stroud to visit Commander Godman (he was now routinely using his old Navy title), and described him as his "Fascist Administrator for Gloucestershire". Godman seemed to thrive on conflict judging by the numerous reports

Röhr-Junior chassis 1933 with its impressive independent suspension system.

in the local papers throughout the Thirties ranging from anti-Semitic propaganda to visiting the Bristol Fascists' branch, with his bodyguard, and tearing down all the papers from their wall because of a policy disagreement. Had Thomas Godman and some of his predecessors carefully preserved all the paperwork from the 1920's and delivered it safely to the Stroud Museum, we would probably have all been much wiser but, sadly, I suspect Albert Lock, the gardener at Cainscross House, eventually had a few very large bonfires.

Hans Röhr's company was re-formed with the help of Swiss financiers and re-named "Neue Röhr Werke AG" on the same site. Ernst Decker was technical director and Hans moved away to carry out design work for Adler. The Thirties were turbulent times for the German motor industry and the new Röhr company weathered many crises before it ceased to exist prior to the War. Its most successful car during this time was the Röhr Junior, based on a Tatra licence. Werner Schollenberger's book, referred to earlier, deals with this era in fascinating detail. Hans Röhr died in 1937, the year in which he came to London to receive the Crompton Medal for his contribution to automobile engineering.

Much later in the early years of the Second World War, Thomas Godman turned to journalism and had at least two full page articles published in The Sunday Pictorial. Whilst propaganda was a regular feature of the war time Press, it is intriguing to read of his exploits and association with the Nazi regime - but that's another story.

Finally, it seems interesting to note that our story begins and ends with a straight eight engine: the Weigel in 1905 and the Röhr engine in 1933.

Left to Right: W. Cheesman, Commander Thomas Godman, Sir Oswald Mosley, Commander Piercey (National Defence Force) and J.W.R. Hopkins (O.C. Stroud).

HITLER'S LIFE WAS IN MY H

THE Englishman playing a lone hand in Ger many certainly sees life. I have bee shadowed by the Gestapo, arrested by ther grilled by them. My telephone wires have be tapped and my mail cleverly opened.

I have been requested quietly but firmly quit Germany for the benefit of my health. at other times, I have sat for hours with the h est officers of the High Command, listenin their plans of campaign and their endless cussions of strategy.

I have sat in Hitler's own box at those enormous Berlin parades and I have been shown the secrets of the Nazis' mighty oil-from-coal plants in the Ruhr.

In my twenty years in Germany I got to know the mind of the Nazi. I had to study the species, and I can claim to know its strengths and weaknesses, its powers and ambitions. I know the Gang Bosses, and the Nazi "boys in the back room," too, the ones the outside world hears little about, but who wield immense power inside Nazidom.

When I went back to Germany after the Nazis were firmly in the saddle the first thing I noticed was that the Big Shots—including my old Beer Cellar pals—

TRUE TO GANGSTER PRACTICE HAD SURROUNDED THEMSELVES WITH BODYGUARDS AND GUNMEN, AND EVEN THE SWANKIEST LITTLE SHOTS NEVER WENT AROUND WITHOUT A COUPLE OF ARMED SUBORDINATES.

By Lt.-Comdr. THOMAS GODMAN, [illegible]

He knew the [illegible] early days and [illegible] only man wh[illegible] negotiate big [illegible] deals with [illegible] behalf of oth[illegible] ments

It was all ver[illegible] illuminating to [illegible] The idea, of [illegible] make themselve[illegible] like. In this co[illegible] like to emphas[illegible] claim to be [illegible] Hitler."

No man [illegible] claim that.

ADOLF [illegible] had a [illegible] in any sha[illegible]

£100 MUST BE WON

Closing Date APRIL 24.

SUNDAY PICTORIAL, April 13, 1941. PAGE 7

INSIDE THE NAZI RACKET

I WAS GOERING'S GUN-RUNNER!

● Here for the first time is the astonishing story of the huge rackets worked by the Nazis. How they bootlegged champagne to raise cash, ran guns to China for scrap steel, blackmailed the world for the lives of wealthy prisoners.

Lieutenant-Commander Thomas Godman, ex-merchant service salesman, ex-submarine officer, a tough adventurous Englishman, who has been inside Germany for twenty years.

THE MORNING WAS BRIGHT, SUNNY, AND WARM AS I STROLLED ALONG BERLIN'S FRIEDRICHSTRASSE.

I was on my way to a late Sunday morning breakfast at a favourite cafe where you could sit and watch the never-ending stream of people—and the never-ending Nazi parades—passing by.

By Lieut.-Commander THOMAS GODMAN R.N.R.

The only Englishman who has known the Nazi leaders since their early days.

He put through huge deals with them, acted as intermediary between them and foreign governments. He watched them at work—and at play. Now he tells the terrific story of the greatest gangsters in the world.

Today Berlin was strangely quiet and broody. The tense atmosphere seemed charged with hysteria—and a hint of terror.

That was Sunday September 3, 1939.

I was thinking over my own strange fortunes and adventures and wondering if my £7,000,000 Arms-to-China deal would go through all right.

At the corner where the Friedrichstrasse crosses Unter-den-Linden, one of Berlin's most famous spots, I halted for the traffic lights.

The end of all thinking, wondering, and hoping came with a whisper in my ear:

"Herr Godman, it is war. They are looking for you ..."

She was the girl friend of one of Goering's henchmen. I caught a glimpse of a friendly, anxious face, heard a whispered "Auf wiedersehen," and she was gone.

In a life like mine the wavering decision can bring unpleasant consequences, so I have learned to obey the instinctive impulse.

At that moment the impulse told me to keep going.

I needed a swift getaway!

As the traffic lights changed the way was open before me, down the Friedrichstrasse, which leads to the Templehof flying field. There were "possibilities" there.

Templehof was the Tom Tiddler's ground of the sporting flying men of Europe. Many of them were my friends.

I have left hats, coats, baggage and effects in many parts of the world when the necessity arose for a swift getaway.

So once again, with all my baggage back in my hotel, without hat or coat, I walked on, quickly but without too obvious a hurry, and sauntered out on to the tarmac of the Templehof.

I paused to admire the lines of a French sports plane, with engine ticking over, and pilot standing by. We exchanged long meaning looks. The French pilot jerked his head. I wedged myself into the second seat, and we jumped into the air like a frightened stag.

We came down on Brussels airport to learn that war had begun.

✦ ✦ ✦

ONE of the things I'd left behind in Nazi Germany was that perfectly good business deal in arms worth some £7,000,000, which meant a lot of commission to me!

The history of the deal throws a very revealing light on to the mentality of the Nazis.

It all began when in round-about ways I was asked to travel to Paris from Berlin to talk with emissaries of the Chinese Government. They wanted arms for their war against the Japs, and they thought I was the man who could obtain them.

It was known, I presume, that I had once run a cargo of arms to the rebel Riffs in Morocco.

At any rate in Paris there began a strange international deal that later involved banks, arms works and Government Departments in Berlin, Washington and London.

The final set-up was that the Germans would supply 400,000 rifles, complete with bayonets, and 1,000 rounds of ammunition each, in return for 640,000 tons of American steel scrap.

There was one little point. The arms were for China, and Germany was the ally of Japan!

Goering wanted steel scrap badly. He was obviously prepared to go to any lengths to get it.

I leaned across his desk in the course of our arguments and said:

"But who do you think wants 400,000 rifles?

"I don't know or care. Who does?" said Goering impatiently.

"The Chinese," I answered.

"All right, what then?" growled Goering.

"Well, what about the Japanese?"

Hermann Goering uttered a short, sharp expletive.

"I want that steel. You get it," he said.

"All right. I want a clearance through Customs for those rifles via Helsinki, and no questions asked or answered."

"You shall have it. Go ahead and finish the deal," answered Goering.

✦ ✦ ✦

NOW it was all gone. But at least I knew the Nazi racketeers well enough to be able to give our own Government a great deal of inside stuff about them.

It was queer how I, a pre-1914 Merchant Navy man, then a submarine navigating officer, came to know first Goering and then the rest of them.

In 1921 I was in Munich, a freelance business adventurer, keeping my eyes and ears open, asking no favours, no protection, seeking no sanctuary.

Germany was a troubled, feverish, crazy country, floundering in the backwash of war, with turmoil, riots, fights, brawls and plottings everywhere.

One evening I was sitting in a Munich beer garden with a nice big beer and idly listening to the usual argument and noise around me, interspersed with the usual phrases like "Rohte fahne" (red flag), "Versailles diktat," "Kommunisten."

THEN THE INEVITABLE SCRAP GOT GOING, SWUNG AROUND MY TABLE, AND BANG WENT MY BEER.

It wasn't a joke any longer, and I soon found myself cracking heads with a garden chair on behalf of a small gang who were having a rough time against superior numbers.

"Police," yelled a dozen voices.

A little man in a dirty coat

One of the scrappers grabbed me and dragged me along with them, out of a back door and along to another beer cellar called the "Gnomenkeller"—the cellar of the gnomes.

There we dusted ourselves off, and called for beer. The young man who had yanked me out of the cafe said:

"We're holding a meeting of our new party here tonight. Our speaker is arriving soon. Why don't you stay and listen to him."

"Oh, politics are not in my line. Anyway, thanks for the scrap," I answered.

"No, you stay. What will you drink? Have what you like."

"Well, if I have to listen to any more of your people's cock-eyed political meetings I'll have nothing less than champagne," I said with a grin.

Just then the door opened and in marched a little man dressed in a seedy raincoat. He had a dishevelled lock of hair falling over his forehead and a big black moustache. He had wild fanatic eyes, and a fidgety manner. I guessed him to be about thirty years old.

Pretty soon the Gnomenkeller was filled to overflowing. I was bored, thirsty and anxious to get away, but the little man in the seedy raincoat was now speaking, in a harsh throaty voice.

As he was well wound-up and did not look like stopping, I leaned across the table to my newly-met brawl acquaintance and said:

"What about that champagne? I'm thirsty."

The blond German laughed and yelled across the room: "Hey, this damned Englishman says he must have a drink now."

The speaker stopped, glowered, and then said in a plaintive voice, "Why do you interrupt my speech like that?"

To my relief the champagne arrived. Glasses were filled, we drank. I nodded across the table to my "host" and said:

"The name's Godman."

"Yah? Fighting man, eh?"

"Sure, submarine officer."

"Yah? My name's Hermann Goering. I'm a flyer."

"Fighting man, eh?" I answered.

"Yes, a fighting man."

We had a few more drinks, the little man's speech went on. We had a lot more drinks.

I leaned across to the man named Goering, and jerking a thumb at the speaker, said:

"What's his name?"

"Him? Adolf Hitler," answered Goering.

✦ ✦ ✦

I GOT the impression in those early days that the Nazi leaders were the German counterpart of the American gangsters.

By gangster I do not mean a back-alley crook or razor-expert. I mean Big Shots, operators on an international scale, ruthless, crooked, cynical, but full of imagination and energy.

AND I KNOW THE GANGSTER TYPE WELL. SOME OF MY YEARS OF ADVENTURE WERE SPENT IN THE RUM-RUNNING BUSINESS FROM GERMANY TO THE UNITED STATES:

The comparison struck me very forcibly a few years later when I watched one of the leading suppliers of bootleg liquor to America become a leading Nazi.

His name was Ribbentrop.

I knew of him in the old days, when he was a champagne salesman, agent for French champagne in Germany and England.

I had indirect dealings with him later in a little matter of smuggling champagne and other liquor into prohibition America.

He did not take an active role in the game. Oh dear no! One saw his agents in elegant offices in London's West End, or in Berlin, and made all arrangements. But Ribbentrop made the money.

I noticed that Hitler seemed to think a lot of his new man. At one party in particular I heard him say:

"You are, there's Ribbentrop. A clever man. He speaks four languages."

It makes me chuckle when I think of Ribbo's career, from the days when he was seeking contacts with the big shots of the bootleg business, men who would buy his liquor by the thousands of cases, to the present day, when he is Germany's Foreign Minister.

NEXT WEEK Your Money for Their Lives

Godman's war effort!

10
Epilogue - So this was Hampton Cars

1923 Hampton 4 seater tourer

I have enjoyed telling this story in which I started out as the compiler, developed into a researcher, historian, commentator, editor and finally it seems - an author. I sincerely hope that everyone who reads this book will learn almost as much as I have about the fascinating history of the Hampton Car and the people who made them.

Whilst serious motoring enthusiasts will easily be able to slot this story into the motoring scene of the Nineteen Twenties, I wish to enlarge a little on the background against which the various Hampton companies were operating for the benefit of more general readers. Jonathan Wood's excellent book "Wheels of Misfortune" chronicles the British Motor Industry from 1896 and his coverage of the Twenties puts our subject into perspective and at the same time helps to answer the most frequent question I have been asked, namely, Why did Hamptons fail? Jonathan tells us that in 1922 there had been 91 makes of British cars on the market which was reduced to only 41 by 1929. In 1923 UK. car production was 71,396 which rose to 182,347 in 1929 with Morris, Austin and Singer having three quarters of this market. As Morris and Austin were operating just over 50 miles away from Dudbridge at Cowley and Longbridge they were without doubt Hampton's major competitors, particularly Morris. A glance at the 1925 Olympia Motor Show catalogue reveals 28 firms offering vehicles in the £300/£400 price range, many with 12 hp models which could be considered as Hampton's competitors.

Competitors at the 1925 Motor Show

A.C.	Calcott	Lea Francis	Swift
Austin	Calthorpe	Morris	Triumph
Arrol-Johnson	Clyno	Rhode	Trojan
Bayliss Thomas	Galloway	Riley	Vulcan
Bean	G.W.K.	Rover	Westcar
Clarke-Cluley	Hillman	Singer	Windsor
Eric Campbell	Humber	Standard	Wolseley

A detailed comparison of the Hampton with its competitors is way beyond the scope of this treatise but I firmly believe that the majority of Hampton Companies consistently built a good, reliable, well-engineered car - perhaps too good for the price levels of the day. However, whilst the market place was tough, what did Hamptons offer that some of the leaders did not? Principally, they used overhead valve engines throughout their production plus a four speed gearbox for most of the time whilst many of the mass producers were only supplying side valve units with three speed gearboxes. It is sobering to note that Ford did not offer an overhead valve engine or four speed gearbox on their family cars until the late 1950's (105E Anglia).

Whilst Hampton's management was consistently striving to improve their product, Morris, Austin and Ford for example were always looking to lower their costs by a combination of mass production, component importation and simplified engineering methods. Just one example relates to the position of the gear change lever. Many companies moved this to the central position but Hampton stayed with their well-established right hand

mechanism which had more working parts and was more expensive to produce. Meadows did offer a cheaper gearbox with centre change but Hamptons declined to incorporate it into their cars. Leaving competition aside, it appears that one of the major causes which contributed to Hampton's eventual failure was that they were totally under financed for what was both a capital and labour intensive industry. Investors in motor companies in general need to be very patient and unfortunately most of Hampton's were not. Whilst they all lost money - some significant sums - perhaps they could take a little comfort from the fact that they provided much needed employment in difficult times. However, it must be recognised that each time the Hampton Companies faltered and changed hands it became increasingly difficult to obtain supplies of components, particularly on credit terms. Naturally, customers and dealers also became more apprehensive about the future availability of spares and general support from the factory.

Another question that has frequently been posed is "Did Hamptons have a Golden Era?" This question is partially answered by reference to the vehicle production chart on Page 158. Whilst Sir John Daniel and his Welsh friends made the most cars and gave employment to the largest number of people, the pioneering efforts of William Paddon deserve consideration. Starting from scratch after the war, his production of vehicles was most commendable although we need to bear in mind that most of the bodies were made by sub-contractors, perhaps regardless of cost!

Milward and Leno's Stroud Motor Manufacturing Co. Ltd.'s performance was equally remarkable, bearing in mind they achieved their output in about one and a half years with a smaller workforce but, after their supreme efforts, Hamptons drifted slowly downhill. In my view, the first half of the decade was their best period - their Golden Era.

William Milward's dedication and contribution to the Hampton cause were second to none. It has now become obvious to me that because William and particularly his wife, Margaret, handed over much useful material concerning Hamptons to Max and Bonnie our story is much more complete - perhaps a lesson to everyone.

The only particular disappointment for me during my research was not to unearth any specific evidence of Hampton's export achievements. If this book reaches some of the outposts of the old British Empire I would be delighted to receive any information concerning Hamptons, e.g. advertisements, press reports or, better still, photos of Hamptons abroad. It would be too much to expect for another Hampton car to emerge after all this time - or would it?

As outlined earlier in the book, written records from within the Hampton Companies have been rather sparse with the exception of sales brochures. However, perhaps by way of compensation, I have gained considerable satisfaction from being able to include a wide variety of pictures which I believe make the Hampton Story both informative and interesting. Selecting these has been something of a challenge but I trust the ones chosen enhance the reader's understanding and enjoyment. Whilst the opportunity to use photographs from many sources has proved invaluable, a special word of appreciation must go to Ken Archibald who kindly loaned the Max Williamson Collection of Hampton material on which I have drawn extensively. Although I only met Max on a couple of occasions over 30 years ago, Ruby, his widow, has shown genuine interest in my work in

recent times. The Bonnie Monro archive is now safely in my ownership. Perhaps surprisingly no photographs of the interior of the final factory were contained in either Max's or Bonnie's collections and unfortunately none has come to light from other sources.

The Hampton Selsley Hill factory is no more but Sainsbury's are to be congratulated for commissioning an attractive illustrated plaque which is prominently displayed on their Dudbridge supermarket. This chronicles the industrial heritage of the site, including information concerning the Hampton Car - a true memorial at last. I am prompted by this to issue a challenge to all the Hampton owners to celebrate the Millenium in style by driving their vehicles to a meeting at Dudbridge on a suitable day. I'm sure they would receive a very warm welcome.

At this point my special thanks are due to Terry Cripps of TCDB. Design and to Cotswold Printing Co. Ltd. for their patience and creative contributions to this book. Terry's ability to interpret my innermost thoughts and to integrate the illustrations in an imaginative way is very much appreciated.

As mentioned in the preface, Keith Stimson has been involved with this project from the very beginning and has continued to provide help, encouragement and many hours of proof-reading which have been invaluable.

Joyce Thomas had the unenviable task of teaching English to both my children at Minchinhampton School some years ago. I was delighted when, despite this experience, she readily agreed to read my draft. My later request to contribute introductory information to be used on the jacket was met with equal enthusiasm for which I am extremely grateful.

Kate LeWorthy, Administration Manager at ARB, has been deeply involved with all aspects of the book from the onset. Her management and data preparation skills have contributed significantly to the project, aided by Karen Townsend with whom she has liaised on the original text creation. Kate's enthusiasm, dedication and hard work have been an inspiration to everyone involved for which I can only offer my sincere thanks.

Having now photographed and evaluated all the known surviving Hamptons, visited all the sites/buildings in which they were made, worked for three years in their old office block and finally produced most of this book in the very building in which their final sales brochures were printed, it is perhaps not surprising that I have developed a certain empathy with the marque. As over one hundred bricks from the walls of the old Hampton factory are now built into our garden patio, I have an additional permanent reminder of Hampton Cars.

Finally, as I pen these last few lines sitting on the well worn seat of Bonnie Monro's old Hampton, which now resides in my garage, I sense that HW 2734 is almost pleading with me to finish this sentence and devote some time to her. On the other hand Joy, my wife, must have similar feelings but to her great credit has not expressed them. Like most cars, Hamptons provide enjoyable transport but this unique vehicle is looking forward to being driven around the Stroud Valleys and making friends with the relatives of those who built her.

Trevor G. Picken

ESTIMATED ANNUAL PRODUCTION OF HAMPTON CARS - FROM THE DUDBRIDGE FACTORIES.
BASED ON ENGINE MANUFACTURERS' RECORDS.

ENGINE MAKE BORE x STROKE CAPACITY	1919	1920	1921	1922	1923	1924	1925	1926	1927	1928	1929	1930	1931-3	TOTALS
DORMAN 63 x 120 mm 1496 c.c.	10	211	25											246
DORMAN 69 x 120 mm 1795 c.c.		24	62	28										114
MEADOWS 63 x 100 mm 1247 c.c.				7	179	136	21			16	16	11		386
MEADOWS 69 x 100 mm 1490 c.c.				55	56	4	104	38	25	11	14	12		319
MEADOWS 75 x 120 mm 2120 c.c.						3	8							11
MEADOWS 72.5 x 120 mm 2973 c.c. (6)											1	4		5
ROHR 60 x 100 mm 2.262 c.c. (8)													1	1
CONTINENTAL 67 x 114 mm 2414 c.c. (6)													2	2
TOTALS	10	235	87	90	235	143	133	38	25	27	31	27	3	1084

COMPANY	HAMPTON ENGINEERING	HAMPTON ENGINEERING (1920)	STROUD MOTOR MFG.	HAMPTON CARS (LONDON)	GODMAN SAFETY SUSP
OUTPUT	245	514	190	132	3

The table gives a general indication of cars produced. However,it is known that occasionally Hamptons fitted other engines -some at customers' request (e.g.Anzani) and a few Meadows engines had the Brooklands specification.

There were rumours that the company designed and produced an engine of their own at some stage, but no evidence of this has come to light. Perhaps it was a prototype which they could not afford to manufacture because of the high cost of initial tooling. The 1683c.c. 6 cyl. engine advertised in 1928 is a mystery, but it is possible that a few cars were made with this power unit.

Allowing for some of these specials it is most unlikely that Hampton's Dudbridge total production exceeded eleven hundred. Unfortunately it is not possible to give a breakdown of which particular models or body styles were sold.

Printing Testimonials from satisfied customers in sales brochures was a popular idea in the Twenties - here is what a few Hampton users said in 1922/23. Their authenticity must be taken on trust.

I have run mine over 1,300 miles already and have had nothing go wrong with her with the exception of one puncture. She races up all the hills with the greatest of ease. She is delightful to drive and most satisfactory in every way. All my friends say she is the most attractive light car to look at they have ever seen.

Enclosed please find cheque for repairs to radiator. I am much obliged for your promptitude on this occasion. The car, I may say, after 8,000 miles is running splendidly. I have had 23 cars of different kinds, sizes and makes, but none of these have been so easy and delightful in their steering as the Hampton. She is "tres douce" in this respect. I have driven the car from Gloucestershire to Windermere and only twice came off the top gear, this would only have been once (had I taken the direct road in Kendal); all other hills were taken by the 11/34 on top with ease. During this inclement winter the Allweather body has been most efficient and a great comfort.

The two 9.8 cars which we purchased from you about nine months ago have given the greatest satisfaction and we think it fair to you to state that with very few adjustments the cars have respectively run between 10,000 and 12,000 miles each without the slightest hitch.

The economy in petrol and oil has been very marked and we can safely say that the Hampton car for travellers' requirements is absolutely the best on the market.

With reference to my new car, I must inform you how pleased I am with this. The springing, smooth running, speed and everything connected with the car is really exceptional. I must say I have never driven a sweeter car and I think it is the last word in two seaters and I hope you will continue to keep the cars up to the pitch you have them now. I have not worked out the petrol consumption carefully but will let you know later what I get out of her to the gallon.

You will be interested to know how the Hampton car I bought from Mr. Ingleby has behaved on a 1,200 mile tour through the Western Highlands of Scotland. Our search for the most interesting scenery took us off the beaten track with the result that we were sometimes faced with severe climbs. For instance:

Cockbridge	1 in 5 to 1 in 9
Lecht Hill	1 in 7
Bridge of Avon	1 in 5
Bridge of Brown	1 in 9 average
Rest and be Thankful Hill	1 in 7

The above figures are from the Royal Scottish Automobile Club and these hills are included in their reliability tests. They are all long climbs, sharp bends and a surface that is simply appalling. Most tourists, I later discovered fight shy of them and no wonder. The Hampton, however, took them all with ease. I started them all on third, dropping to second when the pinch came and on this gear we always had something to spare. With two passengers and luggage, the Hampton simply ploughed its way through the scree and boulders, without over-heating or showing signs of strain.

I am writing to let you know how pleased I am with the Hampton sporting two-seater you supplied me with last January. It is quite the best and the nicest small car I have ever been in.

ACKNOWLEDGEMENTS

The Hampton Workforce

Miss Abdella
Mrs. Grace Blanche
Miss Amy Guest
Mrs. Peggy Ollerenshaw (Née Lodge)
Mrs."Pops" Stimson (Née Joel)
Miss Dene Webb

Les Bassett
Harry Baxter
Bert Brinkworth
Ken Carter
William Cowley
Harry Davis
Mr. Dawkins
Billy Dow
Morton Dudbridge
Jim Durrant
Edgar Fowles
Mr. Friar
Martin Fussey
Norman Greening
Percy Hall
Harold Harmer
Billy Jakes
Ron Johnson
Hector Lithgow
Charlie Milne
Cyril Minett
Harry Minett
Albert Moore
Frank Pick
Frank Poole
Mr. Scolefield
Fred Taylor
Harry Tremelling
Mr. Turner
Sid Vanstone
Albert Waite
Fred Waite
Alf White
Fred Wood

and many others whose names did not emerge during the research.

Workers & Management in Carnival Mood - about 1924. A Hampton car beneath the aeroplane at either Stroud or Cainscross Show.

ACKNOWLEDGEMENTS

ORGANISATIONS

Achievements Ltd. - Heraldic Research - A.R.J. Adolph

Birmingham City Local Studies & History Service

British Library

Brooklands Museum Trust Ltd. - Mike Goodall, John Granger, Julian Temple, John Pulford.

Gloucester Records Office

Gloucestershire Society for Industrial Archaeology - Dr.Ray Wilson

Greenwich Maritime Museum

Hampton-in-Arden Society - Mike Bryant

Historic Commercial Vehicle Society - Chris Taylor

Roger McDonald.

Museum of British Road Transport, Coventry - Barry Collins

National Motor Museum, Beaulieu - Jonathan Day, Marie Tièche, Annice Collett

Newspaper Library

Partnership Art Limited

The Patent Office

Public Records Office, Kew.

Science & Society Picture Library, Science Museum, London - Alexander Hayward

Staffordshire Records Office - Elizabeth Street

Stroud Museum - Susan Hayward, Hugh Morrison

Transec - Ortrud Mullett

Wicliffe Motor Co. - John Fincher

INDIVIDUALS

R.C. Archbold

Ken Archibald

John Baker

Rev. Pat Birt

Clive Bond

David Brownjohn

Mrs. Isobel Clarke

Mrs. Alice F. Cook

Ron Crosby

Ivor Davies

George Demidowicz

John Denley

Spencer Elton

Richard A. Fagence

Norman Ford

Mrs. Stanley Gardiner

Reg Hall

Miss Eileen Halliday

Nigel Halls

Tim Harding

Ken Hobbs

Fred & Ian Holmes

Peter Hull

Mrs. Jill Humpidge

Henry Jenner

Gary & Norman Joseph

Mr & Mrs Graham Juniper

John Kitson

Leslie Kitzerow

John Large

Dennis Mason

Michael Mills

Brian Mumford

Mrs. Mary Neale

Mrs. L. Pillinger

Norman Powell

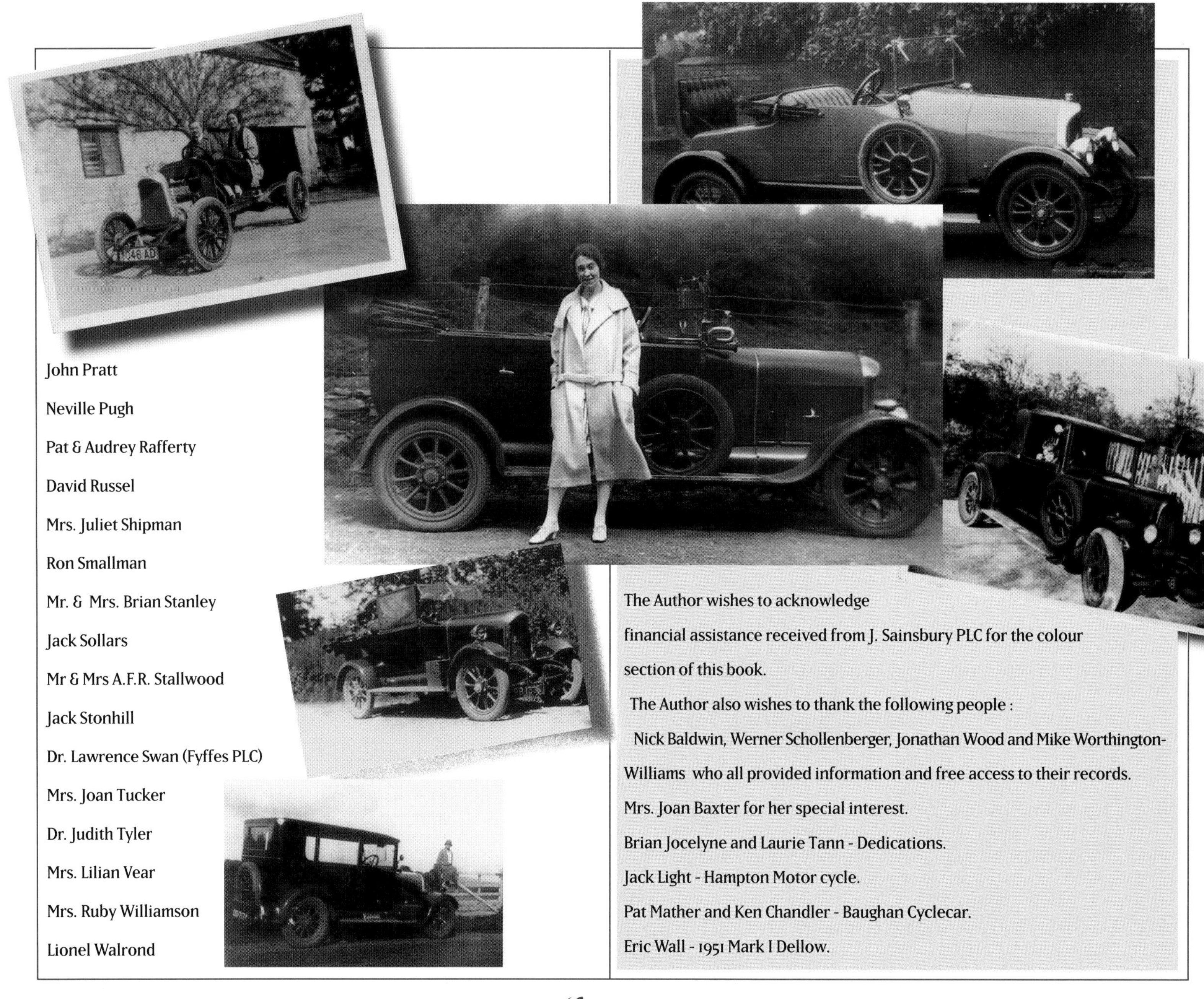
John Pratt

Neville Pugh

Pat & Audrey Rafferty

David Russel

Mrs. Juliet Shipman

Ron Smallman

Mr. & Mrs. Brian Stanley

Jack Sollars

Mr & Mrs A.F.R. Stallwood

Jack Stonhill

Dr. Lawrence Swan (Fyffes PLC)

Mrs. Joan Tucker

Dr. Judith Tyler

Mrs. Lilian Vear

Mrs. Ruby Williamson

Lionel Walrond

The Author wishes to acknowledge financial assistance received from J. Sainsbury PLC for the colour section of this book.

The Author also wishes to thank the following people :

Nick Baldwin, Werner Schollenberger, Jonathan Wood and Mike Worthington-Williams who all provided information and free access to their records.

Mrs. Joan Baxter for her special interest.

Brian Jocelyne and Laurie Tann - Dedications.

Jack Light - Hampton Motor cycle.

Pat Mather and Ken Chandler - Baughan Cyclecar.

Eric Wall - 1951 Mark I Dellow.

PHOTOGRAPHS AND DOCUMENTS

I am indebted to everyone who has loaned photographs and other documents for my use. In some cases the copyright ownership is clear but, in others, the origin is obscure or perhaps claimed by later users who have copied pictures from various sources. Any accidental infringement of copyright is, of course, sincerely regretted. Shown below are the origins we have identified.

J.Atkinson 14, Autocar 84, N. Baldwin 66, Mrs. J. Baxter 103, D. Beedle 134,136, Birmingham Records Library 15, Brooklands Aero Museum 26,31,32, Brooklands Motor Museum 80, N.Bruce 137, M.Bryant, Hampton-in-Arden Society 18,19, Mrs.I.Clarke 98, Mrs.A.Cook 37,49,94, G.Demidowicz 17,18, D.Hales 76, Miss E.Halliday 29,30, T.Harding 87,161 S.Harrison 127, K.Hobbs 109, F.H.Holmes 64, Mrs.J.Humpidge 27, L.Kitzerow 161, Light Car & Cyclecar 72, P. Mather 68,72, McDonald Collection 86, M.Mills 35, Motor Sport 71, Nailsworth Silver Band 71, National Motor Museum,Beaulieu 11,12,13,61,87,100, Mrs.M.Neale 94, Newspaper Library 153, F.Partridge 115, Patent Office 146,147,148, Peckhams 40,153, Mrs.L.Pillinger 16,39, W.Schollenberger 136,138,140,141,142,143,144,145,147,152, Science & Society Picture Library 33, Mrs.J.Shipman 38, K.Stimson 102,104,110,111,113, C.Taylor, HCVS 50,52,53, Dr.J.Tyler 8, Wicliffe Motor Co.10,56,70,73, Max Williamson Collection 7,16,40,46,48,54,56,57,58,59,60,61,62,63,67,74,75,77,78,79,81,83,85,87,88,90,91,96, 97,102,103,105,107,112,145,149,154,159,160,161,162, Mrs.R.Williamson 6, Dr.R.Wilson 55, M.Worthington-Williams 13,25,51,52,81,127

Todays Products FOR YESTERDAYS CARS

Millvale House
Selsley Hill Dudbridge
Stroud Glos GL5 3HF
Tel: 01453 751731
Fax 01453 759630

ARB have been supplying quality components to the older car movement since 1983. They believe their policy of manufacturing and making available many parts to the restoration industry has made a small but positive contribution to preserving many vehicles which might otherwise have found their way to the scrap yard.

The Directors and staff of ARB are pleased to have been associated with this publication.